i want 2 do project.
tell me wat 2 do.

Shakthi Kannan

Published by Shakthi Kannan

ISBN 978-93-5196-738-5

E-mail: author@shakthimaan.com

For further information about this book:
'http://www.shakthimaan.com/what-to-do.html'

Dedicated to my aunt,
Dr. (Mrs.) S. S. Kodimani

Short Contents

Table of Contents

3   Project Communication 31

4   Project Guidelines 42

5   Development Guidelines........52

6   Methodology of Work 67

9 Art of Making Presentations .. 100

10 Sustenance 109

Preface

Why

Free and open source software is a software whose source code is available under a freely distributable license. The license allows you to use, copy, and make changes to the software. This is different from a proprietary software, where you only receive an executable under a restrictive license, and the source code is not provided to you. This is also different from freeware, where the executables are given away for free, without the source code.

A student sent an e-mail to me on contributing to free and open source software projects with the following:

```
i want 2 do project. tell me wat 2 do.
```

I then began to assess the situation in schools and colleges in India, and found that there was quite a gap between the industry and academia in the use and development of free and open source software. I set out to bridge the gap and create awareness on the same, and also engage the community with it.

The free and open source software movements began primarily in western countries, where the culture is very different from that in India. They are predominantly low-context cultures where individualism is given more importance. There are quite a number of books written on free and open source software, its development, and the community that caters to these societies. But, not all of them are applicable to people in high-context cultures, such as India, where people tend to be in groups. They believe that being associated in an organization with large numbers is considered a high value in society. This book aims to bridge this gap by providing the methodology of working with free and open source software for high-context cultures.

What

A quick summary of the chapters:

- Chapter 1, *Mailing List Guidelines*, addresses the recommended format of sending content to free and open source software mailing lists.

- Chapter 2, *Attention to Detail*, discusses with numerous examples the importance of being alert and attentive at work.

- Chapter 3, *Project Communication*, describes the best practices to be followed in project discussions with your team members.

- Chapter 4, *Project Guidelines*, provides the ideal practices to be followed when working on a project.

- Chapter 5, *Development Guidelines*, lists the various programming practices followed in free and open source software projects.

- Chapter 6, *Methodology of Work*, describes the processes involved in a bug fix, packaging example, and in creating a software patch.

- Chapter 7, *Tools*, provides an overview of the various project-related software tools that you should be familiar with.

- Chapter 8, *Reading and Writing*, gives a list of ways to improve your language skills.

- Chapter 9, *Art of Making Presentations*, discusses the important aspects to remember when creating and delivering presentations.

- Chapter 10, *Sustenance*, outlines the work to be undertaken to maintain a free and open source software ecosystem.

How

I suggest you read the book from the beginning till the end. It has been divided into sections so that you can refer to a specific topic, and use it as a reference manual.

Quotations at the beginning of each chapter have been italicized:

There's only two kinds of players - those who hold on to their nerves and go on to win championships, and those who don't. ~ *Harry Vardon*

Code and quotes in the different chapter sections have been generated using a different font:

```
It is better to have 100 functions operate on one
data structure than to have 10 functions operate
on 10 data structures.
  ~ Alan J. Perlis
```

Command line examples use the Bash environment and at times have been split into multiple lines using the backslash (\) character to fit in a page. For example:

```
$ sudo yum install gcc gcc-c++ flex bison \
    make zlib-devel
```

I have tried to pack a lot of content and still keep the number of pages to a minimum. I hope that you will keep this book handy wherever you go, and also use it for quick reference when you work with free and open source software projects.

Where

I have created a website for the book in my domain:

```
<http://www.shakthimaan.com/what-to-do.html>
```

If you have any comments or suggestions you may write to me at:

```
author@shakthimaan.com
```

Acknowledgements

I would like to thank Kushal Das for allowing me to use mailing list archives for illustrative examples.

Thanks to Karl Berry who patiently answered my queries on GNU Texinfo.

My twin brother, Shivan Kannan, deserves credit for the excellent cover design.

I would also like to thank my father, S Kannan, for reviewing the content.

1 Mailing List Guidelines

Truth and clarity are complementary.

~ Niels Bohr

1.1 Sir, Madam

The use of "Sir" and "Madam" is usually avoided when addressing people. It becomes really annoying, when students use it often. In conversation, for example, they start and finish every sentence with "Sir".

```
"Sir, I have a compilation problem, Sir."

"Sir, how can I install both Windows and Fedora on
the same system, Sir?"
```

As long as the two parties acknowledge that they have mutual respect for each other, the use of titles is to be avoided. Getting the message across is more important.

You should always address people by their first name. Abbreviated titles before names like "Prof.", "Dr." are acceptable though.

1.2 Meaningful subject line

Many a time when sending an e-mail, people do not type anything in the subject line. The e-mail either goes into the spam folder, or gets delivered and the subject line looks like:

```
[none]

(no subject)
```

It is very important to use an appropriate subject line when composing a message. A person must be able to tell the context of the e-mail given the subject line.

1.3 SMS

Short Message Service (SMS) is a text messaging service for mobile communication, and for mobile communication only. It is considered very unprofessional to use SMS language in business or when writing e-mail. I always ask students why they don't write their answers in exams in SMS language. They should probably try it once (and probably it will be their last time too!).

```
"ur lec is very usefull to as,thank u for ur lec
by me and my friends,plz provide knowledge
support to as."
```

The reason that text matter in most books is written in full is because it is legible, easy to read and understand.

Everything has a place and time, and it is important to use the right protocol, at the right place, at the right time, with the right people.

You may not be a native speaker of the English language, but, you must at least use a spell-check on any text that you write. It doesn't matter much if the grammar is incorrect. The above message could have been written as:

```
"Your lecture is very useful to us. Thank you for
your lecture by me and my friends. Please provide
knowledge and support to us."
```

1.4 Continuity

```
"i am a fresh computer science enggr, i saw ur
website and interest in
linux.......
really i am proud of ur dedication.....
keep in touch"
```

The ellipsis is a series of three dots that is added for text that has been omitted. I had asked the student who had written the above, as to why so many dots were used, and the reply was that he was thinking at that point of time. It doesn't mean anything to the reader on what the author was doing when writing the e-mail.

If you are quoting a paragraph, and you want to omit irrelevant text, you can use ellipsis. Otherwise, always end a sentence with a full-stop, and start a new sentence with a capital letter. The above e-mail message could have been written as:

```
"I am a fresh computer science engineer. I saw
your website and interest in Linux. I am proud
of your dedication.
Keep in touch."
```

1.5 Capital Letters

```
"HOW TO TRACE C CODE - ANY SUGGESTION?"
```

Newbies assume that writing in capital letters means that they are emphasizing the importance of the text. In Internet forums and mailing lists, text in capital letters means that the person is shouting the sentence at whoever is reading it. Acronyms are exceptions, but, please avoid typing the entire text in capital letters. The above subject line should have been written as:

```
"How to trace C code - any suggestion?"
```

1.6 Top-posting

The method of posting style in mailing lists and forums has been debated for years. The preferred method of style used in free and open source software mailing lists is interleaved, trimmed, bottom-posting.

Top-posting is when you write your answer above the question in your exams (don't try it!). The following individual has top-posted:

Or else you could install kaffeine rather
than xchat.

On 8 July 2011 18:59, a b <abc at gmail.com> wrote:
>
>
> On Fri, Jul 8, 2011 at 4:02 PM, x y <xyz at
> gmail.com>wrote:
>
>> hi Everyone
>> this is x y from foo...
>> in irc my nick is xyz.
>> My problem is very surprising though it is true.
>> my problem is that : in #foo, on class time when
>> pqr give his dialogue at class;that not appear
>> to my irc client (xchat or in xchat-gnome).
>> For that i can see pqr is available although
>> when he say something it not comes to my
>> laptop screen.
>>
>> For information i would like to say: i am using
>> ubuntu 9.10. i have
>> already reinstalled xchat twice.
>> please suggest to get me out from this problem.
>> thank you.
>> ##i am very much surprised : why it is occurring
>> with pqr and me!
>> --
>> Users mailing list
>> Users at lists.mno.org
>> http://lists.mno.org/listinfo.cgi/users-mno.org
>>
> if you are having mozilla than you probably would
> want this https://*addons*.*mozilla*.org/en-US/
> firefox/*addon*/chatzilla/. I think this would
> solve your problem
> regards
> xyz

A person who follows bottom-posting scrolls down to
the end of the message to realize that the person has actually

top-posted. Bottom-posting is when you write your answer
below the question. There are e-mail clients that by default
follow top-posting style. You need to change their setting to
use bottom-posting. But, just that isn't sufficient as shown
in the following reply:

```
On 7/8/13, x y <xyz at gmail.com> wrote:
> First install the dependencies:
>
>  To install dependencies: become root ($ su -)
>  in Ubuntu ($ sudo -s)
>  # git clone git://github.com/xyz/requests.git
>  # cd requests
>  # python setup.py install
>
> THEN:
>
> 1. Become root ($ su -) in Ubuntu ($ sudo -s)
>    DONT if you are already root
> 2. cd /usr/bin/
> 3. wget http://xyz.in/tmp/submit_hometask
> 4. chmod +x /usr/bin/submit_hometask
> 5. exit from the root account (press Ctrl+d)
>
> 6. Now from your normal user account create a
> file called ~/.foo.conf
> Paste the text bellow in that file:
>
> [foo]
> user=
> password=
>
> 7. Add your github username after user=
> It will look like:
> user=foo
>
> 8. reply to this email directly to me with
> your username. I will send a personal email
> with the password.
>
> Foo
```

```
> --
> Users mailing list
> Users at lists.mno.org
> http://lists.mno.org/listinfo.cgi/users-mno.org
>
Hi,
My github username=abc

regards,
ABC
```

The above reply is a bottom-post, but, the author has not trimmed the message. Interleaved, trimmed, bottom-posting is the preferred approach where you remove irrelevant text in the reply, quote only what is relevant to your reply, and reply below the quoted text. The above reply should have been:

```
Hi,

--- On 7/8/13, x y <xyz at gmail.com> wrote:
> 8. reply to this email directly to me with
> your username.

My github username=abc

regards,
ABC
```

1.7 Over-quoting

```
On 28/03/07, foo b <foo b at gmail.com> wrote:
>
> On 3/27/07, xyz f <xyz f at gmail.com> wrote:
>>
>> No..i didnt installed it ...
>>
>>>> Can any one kindly help me to start the
>>>> ssh service.
```

```
>>>>
>>>> FYI: Here is /etc/ssh/ssh_config file content
```

When replying to an e-mail, if you leave a big trail of the previous replies, the reply-to (">") character gets appended as seen above. This can get big for long conversations, and difficult to follow. Hence, avoid large over-quoting of messages. Just quote what is relevant to the context, and reply to the same.

1.8 No HTML messages

```
<html>
<body>
<div style="color:#000; background-color:#fff;
     font-family:arial, helvetica, sans-serif;
     font-size:10pt">
<div><span>My git repo url :</span></div>
<div style="color: rgb(0, 0, 0); font-size: 13px;
     font-family: arial, helvetica, sans-serif;
 background-color: transparent; font-style:
     normal;"> <span><br></span></div>
<div style="color: rgb(0, 0, 0); font-size: 13px;
     font-family: arial, helvetica, sans-serif;
 background-color: transparent; font-style:
     normal;"><span><a href="https://github.com/
     Foo/Home_Tasks">https://github.com/Foo/
     Home_Tasks</a><br></span></div>
<div style="color: rgb(0, 0, 0); font-size: 13px;
     font-family: arial, helvetica, sans-serif;
 background-color: transparent; font-style:
     normal;"><br></div>
<div style="color: rgb(0, 0, 0); font-size: 13px;
     font-family: arial, helvetica, sans-serif;
 background-color: transparent; font-style:
     normal;">Foo(nick : foo)</div><div><br></div>
<div dir="ltr"><hr size="1"><font size="2"
     face="Arial"><b><span style="font-weight:bold;
 ">From:</span></b>abc<abc$@$gmail.com><br><b>
     <span style="font-weight: bold;">To:</span>
```

```
</b>users$@$lists.mno.org<br><b><span style=
"font-weight: bold;">Sent:</span></b>Thursday,
July 4, 2013 7:30 AM<br><b><span style=
"font-weight: bold;">Subject: </span></b>Re:
[mno-users] [demo] setup a github repo for home
</div></div></div>
</body>
</html>
```

What is important is the message that is being conveyed and not what formatting you use. If your e-mail client is configured by default to send HTML e-mail, please change the settings to send plain ASCII text. There are a number of HTML e-mail clients available, but, we cannot assume that everyone uses it. Moreover, not everyone is on broadband connection these days, or people may be on the move with a slow mobile connection. Hence, it is important to not send rich text formats, including RTF, that have additional tag elements. Getting the message across is essential.

1.9 No attachments

People tend to send forwards to mailing lists with huge images or text, that are not relevant to the group. There might even be statements in them saying that if you forward these to other people, you might get something useful. The mailing list servers will also rip out any attachments sent to the list. Refrain from sending anything unrelated to the group.

```
On Fri, Jul 5, 2013 at 12:25 PM, abc
<abc at gmail.com> wrote:

> my github url is:-
> https://github.com/abc/repo
> _____
> Users mailing list
> Users at lists.mno.org
> http://lists.mno.org/listinfo.cgi/users-mno.org
>
-------------- next part --------------
An HTML attachment was scrubbed...
```

```
URL: <http://lists.mno.org/pipermail/users-mno.org/
      attachments/20130705/64361145/attachment.htm>
```

1.10 Social networking website

Social networking websites, sometimes ask for your e-mail passwords. They then login to your account, get all your contacts, and send them invites to join their website. The e-mails sent resemble the following:

```
Person X        Person X has Tagged you! :)

Person Y        Person Y wants to share sites
                with you...

Person Z        Person Z left a message for you...
```

If you have subscribed to a mailing list, then such e-mails will be sent to the group as well, because they are part of your contacts list. Be conscious of where you type your passwords, and don't give them away!

1.11 Disclaimers

Depending on the nature of work, and in the interest of the organization you work for, you may or may not use your official e-mail address to participate in free and open source software mailing lists. Some organization e-mail servers attach disclaimers like the one below to every e-mail that is sent from their server. Some of the clauses are not in line with the philosophy and freedom of free and open source software, and hence avoid using your official e-mail address for such discussions.

```
DISCLAIMER: The information contained in this
message is intended only and solely for the
addressed individual or entity indicated in this
message and for the exclusive use of the said
addressed individual or entity indicated in this
message (or responsible for delivery of the message
```

to such person) and may contain legally privileged and confidential information belonging to CompanyName. It must not be printed, read, copied, disclosed, forwarded, distributed or used (in whatsoever manner) by any person other than the addressee. Unauthorized use, disclosure or copying is strictly prohibited and may constitute unlawful act and can possibly attract legal action, civil and/or criminal. The contents of this message need not necessarily reflect or endorse the views of CompanyName on any subject matter. Any action taken or omitted to be taken based on this message is entirely at your risk and neither the originator of this message nor CompanyName takes any responsibility or liability towards the same. Opinions, conclusions and any other information contained in this message that do not relate to the official business of CompanyName shall be understood as neither given nor endorsed by CompanyName or any affiliate of CompanyName. If you have received this message in error, you should destroy this message and may please notify the sender by e-mail. Thank you.

There are other disclaimers that are phrased as:

This e-mail (including any attachments) is intended for the sole use of the intended recipient/s and may contain material that is CONFIDENTIAL AND PRIVATE COMPANY INFORMATION. Any review or reliance by others or copying or distribution or forwarding of any or all of the contents in this message is STRICTLY PROHIBITED. If you are not the intended recipient, please contact the sender by email and delete all copies; your cooperation in this regard is appreciated.

It is you who have subscribed with your official e-mail address. If the organization isn't okay with you using this account, please refrain from using it. If other e-mail services are blocked in your corporate network, then access the mailing lists outside of work. Learning to respect the values and principles of a group will help you become part of what they stand for.

1.12 Digest mode

Digest mode configuration in mailing lists send a summary of all the week's e-mail discussions that were sent to the group. People who don't have time or bandwidth to follow the discussions as and when they happen subscribe to this mode. But, when they have a query or want to post a reply, they need to edit the subject line before sending the e-mail. Otherwise, the people who are subscribed to receive e-mail as and when it is sent, will receive a subject like:

```
Person Z          Re: Users Digest, Vol 63, Issue 4
```

Some people also tend to top-post their reply, and leave the entire trail of the digest.

```
hi this is my repo url https://github.com/rst/foo

On 7/5/13, a b <abc at gmail.com> wrote:
> hi, this is a b.
> My repo url is https://github.com/abc/Training_
> tasks_demo.
>
> On 7/5/13, xyz <xyz at gmail.com> wrote:
>> my github url is https://github.com/xyz/
>> demo/settings
>>
>> On Thu, Jul 4, 2013 at 6:12 PM,
>> <users-request at lists.mno.org> wrote:
>>
>>> Send Users mailing list submissions to
>>>          users at lists.mno.org
>>>
>>> To subscribe or unsubscribe via the World Wide
>>> Web, visit http://lists.mno.org/listinfo.cgi/
>>> users-mno.org or, via email, send a message with
>>> subject or body 'help'
```

```
>>>             to users-request at lists.mno.org
>>>
>>> You can reach the person managing the list at
>>>           users-owner at lists.mno.org
>>>
>>> When replying, please edit your Subject line so
>>> it is more specific than "Re: Contents of
>>> Users digest..."
>>>
>>> Today's Topics:
>>>
>>>     1. [demo] setup a github repo for home tasks
>>>        (Foo)
>>>     2. Setup a github repo (xyz)
>>>     3. Re: [demo] setup a github repo for home
>>>        tasks (bcd)
>>>     4. Re: [demo] setup a github repo for home
>>>         tasks (efg)
>>>
>>> ------------------------------------------------
>>>
>>> Message: 1
>>> Date: Thu, 4 Jul 2013 15:06:44 +0530
>>> From: Foo <foo at gmail.com>
>>> To: users at lists.mno.org
>>> Subject: [foo-users] [demo] setup a github repo
>>>          for home tasks
>>> Message-ID:
>>>         <
>>> foo at mail.gmail.com>
>>> Content-Type: text/plain; charset=UTF-8
>>>
>>> Hi all,
>>>
>>> For the home tasks in the future sessions, one
>>> needs to go through the following steps.
>>>
>>> 1. Create an account in github
>>> 2. Create a new repo for home tasks (name it
>>> properly)
>>> 3. Goto  settings->Service hooks->Webhooks URL
```

```
>>> and the url [1] as a webhook.
>>> 4. create a directory as test1 in the repo.
>>> 5. Inside it add a file called solution.rst
>>> (Example is at [2])
>>> 6. Do a git push
>>> 7. Reply to this email to the list with the git
>>> repo url
>>> 8. Go back to settings->Service hooks->Webhooks
>>> URL and click on Test Hook
>>>
>>> [1] http://foo.com:5000/updatehook/
>>> [2]
>>> https://raw.github.com/foo/studenttest/master/
>>> assignment1/solution.rst
>>>
>>> Foo
>>>
>>> ------------------------------
>>>
>>> Message: 2
>>> Date: Thu, 4 Jul 2013 16:07:47 +0530
>>> From: xyz <xyz at gmail.com>
>>> To: users at lists.mno.org
>>> Subject: [foo-users] Setup a github repo
>>> Message-ID:
>>>          <bcd at mail.gmail.com>
>>> Content-Type: text/plain; charset="iso-8859-1"
>>>
>>> Hello,
>>>
>>> My git repo url [1].
>>>
>>> [1] <https://github.com/bcd/training>
>>> https://github.com/bcd/training
>>>
>>> Thank You
>>> bcd
>>> ------------------------------
>>>
>>> Message: 3
>>> Date: Thu, 4 Jul 2013 11:23:50 +0000 (UTC)
```

```
>>> From: e f <efg at gmail.com>
>>> To: Users at lists.mno.org
>>> Subject: Re: [mno-users] [demo] setup a github
>>> repo for home tasks
>>> Message-ID:
>>>          <
>>> efg at gmail.com
>>> >
>>>
>>> Content-Type: text/plain; charset=UTF-8
>>>
>>> At 4 Jul 2013 09:36:44 +0000 (UTC) from Foo
>>> <foo at gmail.com>:
>>>
>>> >
>>> >Hi all,
>>> >For the home tasks in the future sessions, one
>>> >needs to go through the following steps.
>>> >1. Create an account in github
>>>
>>> Hello,
>>> My git repository url is :
>>> https://github.com/xyz/foo
>>>
>>> Regards,
>>> xyz
>>>
>>> --------------------------------
>>>
>>> Message: 4
>>> Date: Thu, 4 Jul 2013 16:57:12 +0530
>>> From: p q <pqr at gmail.com>
>>> To: users at lists.mno.org
>>> Subject: Re: [mno-users] [demo] setup a github
>>> repo for home tasks
>>> Message-ID:
>>>          <
>>> pqr at mail.gmail.com>
>>> Content-Type: text/plain; charset=ISO-8859-1
>>>
>>> git repo url : https://github.com/pqr/demo.git
```

```
>>>
>>> On 7/4/13, Foo <foo at gmail.com> wrote:
>>> > Hi all,
>>> >
>>> > For the home tasks in the future sessions, one
>>> > needs to go through the following steps.
>>> >
>>> > 1. Create an account in github
>>> > 2. Create a new repo for home tasks (name it
>>> > properly)
>>> > 3. Goto  settings->Service hooks->Webhooks URL
>>> > and the url [1] as a webhook.
>>> > 4. create a directory as test1 in the repo.
>>> > 5. Inside it add a file called solution.rst
>>> > (Example is at [2])
>>> > 6. Do a git push
>>> > 7. Reply to this email to the list with the
>>> > git repo url
>>> > 8. Go back to settings->Service hooks->
>>> > Webhooks URL and click on Test Hook
>>> >
>>> > [1] http://foo.com:5000/updatehook/
>>> > [2]
>>> >
>>> https://raw.github.com/foo/studenttest/master/
>>> assignment1/solution.rst
>>> >
>>> > Foo
>>> > --
>>> >
```

If the reader is following interleaved, trimmed, bottom-posting, then, he/she will scroll all the way down to the bottom of the e-mail to see if there is more text as part of the reply, only to realize that the person has actually top-posted! If you are not sure how to use digest-mode, it is better to avoid using it. Otherwise, please change the subject line, quote whatever is relevant, and bottom-post. The above reply could have been:

```
Person X          Setup a github repo for tasks
```

```
Hi,

--- On 7/8/13, x y <xyz at gmail.com> wrote:
> 7. Reply to this email to the list with the git
> repo url

My repo url is https://github.com/rst/foo

Regards,

xyz
```

1.13 Out of context

A threaded discussion has a series of replies on a topic, and
the replies allow you to follow the conversation in it. Any
query not relevant to the discussion is to be sent as a new
e-mail, with a new subject line. You can fork a discussion,
but, it is better to start a new post for a discussion. Replying
out of context is termed as "thread hijacking". The following
is an example of a reply that is out of context, with spelling
mistakes, and is also a top-post:

```
I am using bsn13g modem for net conection. For that
I am using foo script. But now this foo is not
workin giving some error
""in line 4898 kill 12678"".

On Fri, May 23, 2008 at 9:26 AM, <users-request at
lists.mno.org> wrote:

Hi all,
In case you missed, submit the html hometask using
the submit_hometask command that you use, with a
link to the html file in github in your rst file.
```

1.14 Flooding

A query sent to a mailing list may or may not get answered. It doesn't mean that people haven't read your question. People on the list are volunteers, so, you are not guaranteed with an answer always. It could be that they may not know the answer, or your question was not suitable for the group. This doesn't mean you should send the same e-mail again to the list. You could try in a different mailing list or find a more appropriate forum for your query.

```
Knowledge advances by steps, not by leaps.
    ~ Lord Macaulay
```

1.15 Private e-mails

```
If you wish to converse with me, define your terms.
    ~ Voltaire
```

When someone sees a reply to their post in the mailing list, newbies have a tendency to reply to the author in private. In general, this is not recommended, unless both the parties agree to communicate in private. The purpose of having a discussion in the mailing list is that you can possibly get replies from a wider group of people, than from an individual. Also, if the sender requests that any reply be sent to him/her instead of the list, then you shouldn't reply to the list!

1.16 Tags

```
[Commercial] Java/Lisp Developer Position in Norway

[OT] Effective mentoring programs
```

Most mailing lists are run by volunteers. If you wish to send any job offers that are of commercial interest, please mark the subject line with a "[Commercial]" tag. Off-topic discussions can be marked with "[OT]", but, it is important to keep a tolerant level for the signal-noise ratio.

1.17 Others

Free and open source software is when the code is made available to you in a free and open source software license. There exists free and open source software for proprietary platforms, and it is fine to discuss it as long as the code is available. There is also freeware, where only the binaries are distributed. Just because the binaries run on GNU/Linux, it doesn't mean it is free and open source, and it doesn't mean you can ask the mailing list for support! If you have paid for a proprietary product and support, you are entitled for commercial support. You need to ask your vendor for support, because you are entitled to it. It is inappropriate to discuss queries not related to free and open source software, just because you find many technical people in the list. Every group has its own principles and values - and it is important to know what they believe in.

```
The tension between open source developer needs and
commercial product needs will never go away.
   ~ Eric Allman
```

1.18 References

1. RFC 1855. October 1995. Netiquette Guidelines. https://www.ietf.org/rfc/rfc1855.txt.

2. Fedora Project Mailing List Guidelines. https://fedoraproject.org/wiki/Mailing_list_guidelines.

3. Moen, Rick, & Raymond, Eric S. 2006. How To Ask Questions The Smart Way. http://www.catb.org/~esr/faqs/smart-questions.html.

4. Indian Linux User's Group-Chennai guidelines. http://ilugc.in/mailinglist-guidelines.

5. Debian Community Guidelines. http://people.debian.org/~enrico/dcg/.

2 Attention to Detail

Trifles make perfection, but perfection itself is no trifle.

   ~ Michelangelo

2.1 Who is Deepika?

I once received a request for a Python workshop to be organized at a premier institute:

```
Dear Deepika

Greetings!!!

The IEEE Student Branch of X Institute of Technology,
is organizing a student project contest on 2-3 March,
2008. With the context of our event we wish to have
a two day Python language workshop at our college. I
wish the workshop to cover basic and majorly
requisite portions of python.

Looking for your reply!

Regards,
R
Technical Secretary
IEEE Student Branch
X Institute of Technology
```

I thought that the e-mail was well drafted, except, for the addressee. I sent a reply asking:

```
Who is Deepika?
```

I didn't receive any reply. The initiative and intent of organizing a useful workshop is good. But, please be conscious of whom you are addressing the e-mail to!

2.2 Reply to all

A commercial job posting in a mailing list may request the interested applicants to reply in private with their details. The prospective candidate may not pay attention to it, and send the reply directly to the mailing list. If it contains personal information, then everyone subscribed to the list may read it! The following is an example:

```
RE: REGARDING JOB

Dear sir ,

I am ABC. Very interested to make a good career
with your esteemed organization.Below are my brief
details for your consideration. My detailed resume
can be found as attachment.

Qualification---------MCA 2011 with 61.00 % from
                 Y university

Technical Forte------ASP.Net, C# ,java,SQL-Server,
                 HTML, AJAX , java script,
           j query

Current Location-----------Z

Willing To Relocate-------Yes
ex= 6 month internship
EX =2 month as a jr software developer
total ex = 8 month

Profile = .net developer , database

Joining time----------------With in 10 Days
```

Before sending an e-mail, review the text that you have composed. Also check to whom you are sending the e-mail. Please note that public mailing lists are archived, and hence any content you send may remain forever. Think twice before you say anything or send an e-mail.

2.3 Mentoring questions

I request newbies who want some mentorship to answer the
following questions:

- GNU/Linux distribution currently in use.
- Are you working/studying/any other?
- What are your strengths and weaknesses?
- What is your Internet connectivity type and speed?
- Interested project(s).
- Any prior F/OSS work (provide link).
- What do you see yourself working with, six months down
  the line?
- How much time do you intend to spend on the project
  per week?
- Read and understood "i-want-2-do-project.tell-me-wat-
  2-do" presentation?
- Your skill set (technical/non-technical). List them.
- What are your school and college marks in mathematics?

Many a time, I don't receive answers for most of the
questions. This also happens in threaded conversations in
a mailing list, where some of the questions are skipped.
Answers to all questions are important to provide support or
assistance. Whether the sender got distracted while replying,
or forgot to answer doesn't help the cause. Please double
check your reply to make sure that you have answered all
the questions.

```
You've got to get the fundamentals down, because
otherwise the fancy stuff is not going to work.
   ~ Jim Graham
```

2.4 Submitting after deadline

```
I applied for project X, but missed the deadline to
submit a proposal by 10 minutes.
```

The project did not extend the deadline to the student. Time
is a very important entity. Time lost or wasted cannot be

recovered. Unfortunately, there is no undo button for it. Also, you cannot go back in time to fix things (as of 2013). It is important that you are conscious of where you spend time. There are number of time tracking applications that you can use. Reminder tools can provide you with notifications for time critical tasks. Be aware of deadlines.

2.5 Programming language guidelines

Every programming language has a standard, and a set of guidelines that need to be followed. The GNU coding standard [1] is followed by Free Software projects. A function name and open parenthesis need to start on a new line and on column one:

```
int
main (int argc, char **argv)
{
  return 0;
}
```

A while loop should be indented as follows:

```
#include <stdio.h>

int
main (int argc, char **argv)
{
  int i = 0;

  while (i < 10)
    {
      printf ("%d ", i);
      i++;
    }

  return 0;
}
```

The names of variable names in GNU programs need to be in English, and they have to be meaningful. Local variable names can be shorter because their scope is limited. It is very important to learn to follow the programming language guidelines so that your code is consistent. It also helps others to read and understand your code easily.

2.6 int p,q,r,s,t,u,v

Students have named variables in programs as follows:

```
int p,q,r,s,t,u,v;
```

The variable names should clearly indicate the purpose. You should write code because you feel it is useful to you and also to others who will read your code. Pay attention to how you name your variables, functions, classes etc. You can add comments next to variable declarations if you wish to provide an explanation.

```
You should name a variable using the same care with
which you name a first-born child.
    ~ Robert C. Martin
```

2.7 Return values of functions

There are many library functions that return a status on completion. Many newbies don't necessarily see how library functions are implemented, or read the documentation. As a result, they may not handle an unknown return value. This can affect their program execution when exceptional cases arise. The system() function returns -1 on error. The manual page of system() states the following:

```
RETURN VALUE

The value returned is -1 on error (e.g., fork(2)
failed), and the return status of the command
otherwise. This latter return status is in the
format specified in wait(2). Thus, the exit code of
the command will be WEXIT-STATUS(status). In case
/bin/sh could not be executed, the exit status will
```

be that of a command that does exit(127).

If the value of command is NULL, system() returns
nonzero if the shell is available, and zero if not.

It will be good to check the exit status of a function call.
For example:

```c
#include <stdio.h>

int
main (int argc, char **argv)
{
  int status = 0;

  status = system("whoami");

  if (status == 0)
    printf ("Success!\n");
  else
    printf ("Failure!\n");

  return 0;
}
```

It is also a good practice to read code from libraries and
learn from them. Free and open source software gives you
the freedom to download, study, re-use, distribute and make
modifications to the code.

2.8 Indentation

```c
#include <stdio.h>

int main(int argc, char **argv)
{
int count, i, a=0, b=1, n;

printf("Enter the number of terms: ");
scanf("%d", &count);
```

```
printf("Fibonacci series: ");
for(i=0; i<count; i++)
{
if(i<=1)
n= i;
else
{
n=a+b;
a=b;
b=n;
}
printf("%d ",n);
}
}
```

In many computer lab sessions, I have observed students type their programs completely left-aligned, as illustrated in the above. There is absolutely no indentation, whatsoever. But, the same student who writes the code in an examination, may use some indentation. Why the difference in output from the keyboard and pen? Indentation makes it easy to read code. The source of input does not matter, but, it is important to be uniform throughout. The program could have been indented as follows:

```
#include <stdio.h>

int
main (int argc, char **argv)
{
   int count, i, a=0, b=1, n;

   printf ("Enter the number of terms: ");
   scanf ("%d", &count);

   printf ("Fibonacci series: ");

   for (i=0; i<count; i++)
     {
        if (i<=1)
           n=i;
```

```
      else
        {
          n=a+b;
          a=b;
          b=n;
        }
      printf ("%d ",n);
    }
}
```

2.9 Project guidelines

A free and open source project will also have its own set
of guidelines that you should be familiar with. The Linux
kernel code defines a Tab to have eight characters. The open
parenthesis for an 'if' statement should be at the end of the
line as shown below:

```
if (i > 10) {
    break;
}
```

The methodology to send a Linux kernel patch is also
well documented [2]. It is important that you invest time in
reading and understanding the project documentation before
you start contributing to it. A project may also use a specific
workflow for developers, testers and other team members.
Learning to use them precisely will help you do things as
required by the project.

2.10 Markers F, J

I always ask the following question in my workshops:

```
"Why are there markers on keys F and J on
your keyboard?".
```

I usually get different answers such as:

```
"Manufacturer defect."
```

"I don't know."

"Never noticed them."

The most common answer is:

"To help the blind."

The markers are meant to place your index fingers. Since, most students that I have seen don't know touch typing, they are not familiar with the markers. When you move your hand to the mouse, and return to the keyboard, the marker guides you to place your index fingers and position your hand at the correct keys. It is a reference point from where you can access other keys on the keyboard. Know where your keys are, and learn to touch type.

2.11 Sitting before a computer

In all affairs it's a healthy thing now and then to hang a question mark on the things you have long taken for granted.
    ~ Bertrand Russell

You should learn how to sit before a computer and maintain a good posture. The screen should be at eye level. Your arms must be at right angle and parallel to the floor when using the keyboard. You should sit at least at an arm's length from the screen. You should rest well on the back of the chair and not lean forward. The shoulders should be relaxed. Computer ergonomics is essential to maintain a good posture when using the computer to avoid any discomfort.

2.12 Patience is a virtue

I have interviewed many students. By many, I mean a lot. Most of them tell me that they didn't have enough patience. I wonder if this has anything to do with the "fast-food" culture. There is a lot of difference between speed and being aggressive to getting things done. Speed thrills, but kills. Anything that is learnt in detail and well understood with time spent, will last a life time. Slow and steady always wins the race. It is common among students when they face an error, that they panic and give up. Paying attention to the problem, and analysing it with patience is important.

```
Chance only favours intervention for minds which
are prepared for discoveries by patient study
and persevering efforts.
    ~ Louis Pasteur
```

2.13 Error logs

Students also need to learn to read logs. The log files could be server logs, debugging output, compilation errors, command outputs etc. The outputs are meaningful when posting a problem to a forum. People often only state the problem:

```
hello all
i am facing some problems
1. my bash prompt changed to bash-4.2 $ from the
default how to reset it ?
2. when i edit something by opening files from the
git directory in kword it fails please suggest some
measures so that i can edit and save by kword and
other editors.
```

But, just stating that the car broke down doesn't help the mechanic or automobile engineer to find the cause of the problem. When stating a problem or filing a bug report, it is essential to give detailed inputs - software version, distribution used, steps followed so that others can try to reproduce the problem on their side. Paying attention to the logs can themselves help you identify the problem. This will also greatly improve your troubleshooting skills.

2.14 Attention span

The attention span of the audience in my sessions is 45 minutes. The college classes also have this time period. It is very important to take regular breaks, as your brain needs a rest. The more you try to extend your work timings, the more tiresome you may feel. Taking a break can divert your mind for a short period of time before getting back to what you were doing earlier, and it can bring you fresh ideas. Doing exercises regularly can also help freshen up your mind. There are tools like WorkRave [3] that can remind you when to take a break. The important thing to note here is that you should rest when your body requires it.

```
The first rule of great concentration is
paying attention.
    ~ Tina Konstant
```

2.15 Causes for distraction

```
Most people don't discover how to live until it's
time to die - and that's a shame. Please, don't let
that happen to you.
    ~ Robin Sharma
```

There are many sources of distraction:

- E-mails
- Chat
- Phone calls
- SMS
- Social networking websites
- Meetings
- Television

It takes at least 10 minutes for the human brain to get back to what you were doing prior to the interruption. How does one balance work that needs to get done, and use the various communication channels? Every individual is different and it is important to learn where your weaknesses are. When you want to get work done, disconnect everything else, and aim to finish your work. You can also move to a place where people will not disturb you. This may or may not be possible depending on the location. There are good books that I recommend on Getting Things Done (GTD):

- Stephen R. Covey. "The 7 Habits of Highly Effective People." [4]

- Fergus O'Connell. "How to Get More Done: Seven Days to Achieving More." [5]

Be conscious of where you spend time, how much you spend, and where you need to spend time. Aim, measure, monitor and try to improve your overall productivity.

2.16 References

1. GNU Coding Standards. `http://www.gnu.org/prep/standards/standards.html`.

2. Submitting patches. `https://www.kernel.org/doc/Documentation/SubmittingPatches`.

3. WorkRave. `http://www.workrave.org`.

4. Covey, Stephen R. 2000. *The 7 Habits of Highly Effective People*. Simon & Schuster.

5. O'Connel, Fergus. December 2007. *How to Get More Done: Seven Days to Achieving More*. Prentice Hall.

3 Project Communication

A student's basic skills: ability to apply critical thinking and problem-solving, communicate effectively, and collaborate.

    ˜ Tony Wagner

3.1 No personal questions

```
"Sir, how much salary are you earning?"
```

Working with free and open source software projects has both a technical and a social side to it. When you work with people from different backgrounds, you learn their approach and style of problem solving. But, there is also a social side to it, where, you learn about their cultures and countries. The more you interact with them on Internet Relay Chat (IRC), the more you will learn. You should avoid asking any personal questions though. It takes time to get a rapport among team members and to understand each other. When you have worked with the team members, and only when they are comfortable with you, they can be requested for any personal help.

3.2 Right communication tool

```
To a man with a hammer, everything looks like
a nail.
    ˜ Mark Twain
```

It is very important to learn to use the right communication tool, for the right job, with the right people, at the right time. Sending a Short Message Service (SMS) to your professor may or may not be appropriate, depending on the context and urgency of the situation. The various communication tools have their own unique purpose and reason for existence, and it is thus important to know when to use them in a project. If a mentor is available online on Internet Relay Chat (IRC), it is courteous to ask him if he is free to have a discussion. If there exists a specific feature request that needs to be implemented and you have an idea for the same, it will be better to discuss the same in a project mailing list where all the team members can provide you with feedback. If the discussions become heated up, it will be better to have face-to-face conversations to come to a consensus. If the project team members are spread across the world, then an online video conference can help in resolving any issues. Offline discussions should also be documented in the project wiki for future reference. Learn to not just use the communication tools, but also on when and where to use them.

3.3 Detailed discussion with a mentor

```
There is no royal road to mathematics.
   ~ Menaechmus
```

Before you start work on a project, it is important for you to have a detailed discussion with your mentor. You will need to write to your mentor as to when you intend to discuss the project tasks that you are interested in, and how you plan to solve them. The expectations on both sides must be made very clear. You should decide and agree on how you plan to correspond. If there are project specific tools to use, you need to learn them. If you are not familiar with the software, you need to see which tutorials or manuals need to be followed to learn about them. You should have short-term and long-term goals, and an approximate time-frame to work on them. If you need to gain domain knowledge, you need to prepare a list of the required reading material. The best way to contact the mentor must be agreed upon when you have a problem and not found a solution after doing your homework. It is thus very important for you to take an initiative and discuss everything before you actually begin work on a project.

3.4 Write about yourself

Collaboration is the key in free and open source software projects. When requesting a mentor for guidance, you must write on your skill-set, your areas of interests, the project time-frame that you have in mind and also about yourself. Not everything is technical in a project. Social skills are also equally important. You can also write about your extra-curricular activities, and any voluntary efforts that you have undertaken. These showcase your initiatives and indicate that you are a self-starter. You can provide the link to your website or blog home page, GitHub [1] or Gitorious [2] repository pages, or any other project hosting website where one can see the work that you have done. If you have attended any conferences and have sent event reports of the same, do provide their links. These demonstrate that you are keen on attending events to learn and improve your knowledge. You need to provide enough justification to show that you really want to do the project, and why you must be the one working on it.

```
The social graph is very simple here. Everybody
knows everybody.
     ~ Yossi Vardi
```

3.5 Meeting agenda

```
Say what you mean. Mean what you say.
     ~ Robert C. Martin
```

People working on free and open source software projects may have to balance time between their day job and their voluntary contributions. If you invite them to a meeting, it is important to have an agenda. This becomes even more crucial when people live in different time zones. They may have to attend the meeting at odd hours. People having interest in their work will do so irrespective of the time. But, a clear agenda will help every one list the points of discussion, and any relevant questions that they might want to ask. The minutes of the meeting need to be sent after every meeting with a summary, and it can also be archived for future reference. The list of action items must also be mentioned which need to be followed up subsequently. Time is critical and when you utilize everybody else's time, there must be a meaning and objective in the meeting and it must serve its purpose.

3.6 On time

Whereas symmetry is a property of space, time is
irreversible. Time's arrow distorts symmetry.
    ~ Jean-Claude Risset

Time is a very important entity in this world. If there is
a scheduled meeting at a given time, it is important to be
present before the meeting begins. If it is an online Internet
Relay Chat (IRC) meeting, then make sure your Internet
works and you are logged on to the respective channel at least
five minutes before the meeting. If the project team members
are spread around the world and the meeting is scheduled
in a different time zone, you need to check in advance the
scheduled time as per your location. Some countries follow
Daylight Savings Time (DST) where they forward the time
by an hour in winter and advance it by an hour in spring.
Please double check the meeting timings before you are ready
to attend it. If a blog update needs to be sent by Friday,
midnight 2359 IST, it means that it must be updated before
that time. If you need to submit a project feature by a given
deadline, it needs to be sent before that deadline. Learn to
be punctual and self-disciplined in managing and keeping up
your time.

3.7 Inform in advance

I was busy with exams and unable to do any work for
Fedora or Fedora Sub-Projects.

A student does not send any status update, and one fine day
I get an e-mail that he was busy with his examinations. The
exam dates were not announced overnight. If you are going
on vacation or there is an emergency that you need to attend
to, it is courteous to inform your mentor about it. It is thus
very important to provide regular updates to your team so
that they are well informed of your progress. Taking breaks
or going on a vacation is fine. Just make sure that you have
the relevant documentation in place, so it is easier for you to
recap when you return to work. If a meeting is scheduled on

a specific date, and you are not able to join, send an e-mail to the respective stakeholders. If there is an agenda to discuss and you are not able to make it, then whatever topic that is relevant to you can be taken up when you are present. The important point is to keep everyone informed!

3.8 Before asking a question

```
Better yet, don't ask to be taught - go learn
for yourself.
     ~ Chad Fowler
```

It is very important for you to do your homework and try to find out solutions before asking a question. You can first use a search engine for errors that you get to see if others have faced a similar problem. You can go through the suggestions given in mailing list archives or forum posts that are listed from the search results. If you don't get relevant answers, try to refine your search query. If you still haven't found a solution, you can ask on a project Internet Relay Chat (IRC) channel for help. People may or may not be in front of the computer when you ask a question, and may be away from the keyboard (AFK). People might also be living in different time zones. If you don't get an answer, look for other sources of information. Send an e-mail to the respective project mailing list for help. Avoid sending the same query to multiple mailing lists at the same time. Wait for some time before trying on a different mailing list. Only when none of the above approaches work, should you write to your mentor or code author. Make sure you mention the steps you have taken to solve the problem so that others know the background efforts you have taken, and that you are serious about solving the problem.

3.9 No interest project

```
Follow your passion, not the latest fashion.
     ~ Suhas Patil
```

When students learn about the power of free and open source software, they get very excited about the opportunities it provides. They also want to be a part of it and decide to do a final year project using it to make their presence felt in the community. It is very important to understand why using a particular software or tool is helpful in a project. Some students have no interest in free and open source software and decide to do a project using it because it has a high market value. You should never force yourself to do anything. Whatever is forced on you will not result in a wholehearted effort. It will neither do good for you or the project. People can encourage and motivate you to use free and open source software. But, you must be the one to realize the importance of it. Thus, if you are not fully satisfied and have no interest in it, don't force yourself to work on it. A final year project done without any interest will not be a fruitful free and open source software project.

3.10 No response

Indifference elicits no response. Indifference is not a beginning; it is an end.
    ~ Elie Wiesel

At the end of a presentation, students generally hesitate to ask questions during the Q&A session. Some may do so for the sake of asking a question, but, most of them are too shy. When you are asked a question and there is no response, it either means that you don't know the answer to it, or you feel that getting to know the answer may not be relevant or useful to you. It is very important to be pro-active when working with free and open source software projects, and be eager to solve problems and take in more challenging work. If successive meetings in a project end without any positive responses, or work doesn't get delivered on time, then it is an indication that the team members are losing interest in the project. When there are no weekly updates from students, I ask them for a status update, and they usually don't respond. It means that they haven't done any work and hence they don't want to reply. It is acceptable to inform your mentor in advance that you are busy with other work, and that you will get back to the project work sometime later. Not doing work is fine, but, not being responsive isn't acceptable at any professional level.

3.11 Raise the flag

```
We do not overcome our doubts by suppressing them.
We do not meet our misgivings by denying them.
    ~ Paul Brunton
```

The phrase "raise the flag" means to draw attention to a problem. You should make every effort to solve the problem using the various communication channels before asking your mentor. You should not wait till the deadline and then inform that you are stuck with a problem. The weekly updates are thus very helpful to keep track of your work, and you can raise any issues upfront so that the project team members can guide you accordingly. If there is a problem, try different approaches to solve it and document your findings. Only then should you raise the flag. You can also decide on the time before which you should raise the flag with your mentor prior to starting any project work. When you are a newbie and everything is new to you, it is very easy to give up. But, raising the flag at critical times and following advise can help you climb the steep learning curve.

3.12 Question mark at the end

```
God is in the details.
    ~ Ludwig mies van der Rohe
```

I once had an online conversation with a student where he was making a lot of statements. As I was reading through his statements, he asked me why I was not answering his questions. Every statement that he wrote ended with a full stop. If you are asking a question in a written form of communication, you need to put a question mark at the end of the sentence. This not only applies to Internet Relay Chat (IRC) communication, but, also when writing e-mails. When you speak and wish to ask a question, you end the statement with a different tone so the listener knows that you are asking a question. But, in writing, the only way to indicate a question is by adding a question mark at the end of the sentence. The reader of your text also understands that you are expecting an answer.

3.13 I know C, but, can't understand C projects

A common statement made by students who are getting started with free and open source software projects is:

```
I know C, but, I can't understand the C in
this project.
```

Students are usually asked to write a few hundred lines of code in their college lab work, and they do copy code from their friends and submit the same programs. They are only familiar with the programming style known among their peers. But, in free and open source software projects, code is written by people with different experiences. It is a wonderful opportunity for you to learn from them. It will open up your mind and will also help you look at your existing projects from a new perspective, and how you can improve on them. Given a scale of 1 to 10 (10 being the best), students often rate themselves in programming know-how with a score of 8.0 or 9.0! It is very important to know that there is always something new to be learnt. Peter Norvig said that it takes at least 10 years to master programming [3]. When you move to the development and engineering side of a project, just knowing the syntax and semantics of a programming language isn't sufficient. You also need to know how a problem can best be modelled to solve it. This can be learnt by reading free and open source software code.

3.14 Don't explain the error

```
My Fedora clock is malfunctioning.

What happens is that when I get to the login
screen ... Linux initializes a weird time by itself
```

```
When I compared my Linux's boot with my friend's
Linux's boot .... what I found that during the
black boot screen ........ normally Linux recoeds
the system Date and Time from the BIOS and then
starts and application named UDEV.

But in my case, the first step does not take
place and it directly starts UDEV ......
```

A very common observation is that when newbies face an error, they try and explain the error in their own words. If English is not their native language, it becomes even more difficult for them to express themselves, and also for others to understand what they are trying to convey. While you must provide as much detailed information as possible when posting a problem, try to conform to the technical content. Instead of trying to explain the error, simply paste the error output. Since the source code is readily available ("free as in freedom"), the project team members can locate the code that could have caused the error. The same is applicable when asking questions on Internet Relay Chat (IRC). There are online code pasting services like Pastebin [4], GitHub Gist [5], and Fedora pastebin [6] where you can paste the output and send the URL. This will save considerable time in understanding the problem as compared to having to ask repeated questions to get the required information.

3.15 Panic on GCC error

```
sqrt.c:(.text+0x1c): undefined reference to 'sqrt'
PLEASE HELP!!!
```

Students often panic when they see an error in the output. Life is not fair. Let us accept that. To overcome the fear of errors or failures, it is important to look at a number of them. With experience, you will be able to spot the cause of the error. You should also record the time you spend on a computer doing productive work, without any distractions. Students need to spend quality time doing hands-on work if they wish to learn. Failure is part of the learning process. The more mistakes you make, unknowingly, the more reasoning you can do to fix the same, and better the learning experience. If sqrt.c had the following code:

```
#include <stdio.h>
#include <math.h>

int
main (int argc, char **argv)
{
  int x = 4;

  printf("Square root of %d is %.2f\n", x, sqrt(x));

  return 0;
}
```

If you had tried to compile using:

```
$ gcc sqrt.c

/tmp/cc3SKr6E.o: In function 'main':
sqrt.c:(.text+0x1c): undefined reference to 'sqrt'
collect2: error: ld returned 1 exit status
```

You should not panic and send an e-mail immediately to a mailing list asking for help. Read what the error is and search for answers. You will be building the solution space in your mind as you analyze the problem. The math library is missing in the linking phase, and is thus required to be specified as shown below:

```
$ gcc sqrt.c -lm
```

Try to troubleshoot the problem yourself, and don't panic on seeing the error messages!

3.16 References

1. GitHub. https://github.com/

2. Gitorious. https://gitorious.org/

3. Norvig, Peter. 2001. Teach Yourself Programming in Ten Years. http://norvig.com/21-days.html

4. Pastebin. http://pastebin.com

5. GitHub Gist. https://gist.github.com/

6. Fedora pastebin. http://fpaste.org/

4 Project Guidelines

Adding manpower to a late software project makes it later.
    ~ Brook's Law

4.1 Write abstract, code, documentation and presentations

```
If you really want to do something, you'll find a
way. If you don't, you'll find an excuse.
    ~ Jim Rohn
```

A student approached me for help in creating an abstract for a project. After an initial discussion on his idea, I provided him a brief write up. Few weeks later, he pinged me online on Internet Relay Chat (IRC) for help in coding the project. I had worked out a proof of concept (PoC) implementation for him. Later, the faculty wanted him to write some documentation for the project and he approached me again for help. I wrote a page explaining the idea and citing reasons for the design and implementation. After a month, the student again came back to me asking for a presentation! Mentors are there only to guide you in your project. They cannot write abstract, code, documentation and make presentations for you! Even if you are time bound, you need to learn to plan your work. It is very important to be clear on what you must do and what mentors can do for you. The effort has to come from you, and that is when you actually learn. Self-motivation is thus very important when working with free and open source software projects.

4.2 Small tasks before handling big tasks

```
Little drops of water make the mighty ocean.
    ~ Julia A. Fletcher Carney
```

Newbies with little practical experience can feel daunted by any task given to them. Handling complex problems or making an assessment can be hard. It is thus important to break a task into smaller sub-tasks and work on them individually. You can also request the project team members for beginner tasks to be worked upon stating that you are new to the project. This approach can get you started on a project. Working on smaller problems can also help you understand the tools used in the project and the workflow. It is also convenient for the team members to take time to review and correct smaller mistakes rather than having to go through a larger modification. Correcting smaller mistakes at an early stage is easier than to undo or redo a lot of changes before a project delivery. The scope of smaller tasks also helps you to focus and understand a module, its design and implementation without having to worry about the larger pieces of a project.

4.3 Last minute work

The early bird catcheth the worm.
   ~ John Ray

I always ask a question in my lecture sessions to know how many students study just a few days before an examination. Most of them raise their hands. Some of them ask for important questions that may appear in an examination, and study only those relevant topics. Some students study only to obtain a pass mark and hence feel that whatever is sufficient to study can be done just days before the examination. This approach doesn't work in real life though. To manage your work–life balance, you need to plan early and work systematically. Only this will help you manage both time and resources. If you work every day, sharing the workload over a period of time, you will reap the benefits before a deadline. You will also not feel the burden of it. Any last minute work done under pressure will not be a wholehearted effort, and that will reflect on your work. It will be very obvious. The human body has a biological cycle and rhythm. If you allot time every day for your tasks, you will automatically fall into the cycle of doing work regularly.

Study every day and do your homework daily. Avoid any last minute work!

4.4 Steep learning curve

```
The students should be reaching up to it because
success in life demands the use of intellect
under pressure.
    ~ Bill Cosby
```

The methodology, tools and approach in free and open source software can be entirely new or different from what you are used to. You may not understand everything when you are starting. You will feel frustrated at times. It is very important to be patient, and reason why things do not work the way you expect them to. When you learn to ride a bicycle, you will fall and hurt yourself. Only when you fall, you will learn through your mistakes. The learning curve is very steep. But, learning indeed is hard. It is thus important to persevere and understand if you wish to receive the benefits of free and open source software. If it becomes overwhelming, take a break and do some other work. You can return to the task with a fresh mind, and you may be able to see the problem from a newer perspective. Persist and survive. Everyone has gone through the same steep learning curve, and you are no different.

4.5 No blunt info

```
If you can't explain it simply, you don't
understand it well enough.
    ~ Albert Einstein
```

The free and open source software mailing lists are usually run by volunteers. If you have a problem in your work and need assistance, you must give as much information on the same, stating what you are trying to solve. If you are working on a specific feature request or bug, provide a link to the same. You should give a context to the problem, some background information on the task that you are working, any prior relevant communication with the project team members, the approach you have taken and any errors or output that you have observed. This can serve as documentation for you and others involved in the project. If people face a similar issue in future, a search in the mailing list will return these relevant discussions. Try to give detailed technical information when posting a question related to your work.

4.6 Journal or log of activities

The errors in our own history make us open to new ideas, open to unusual ways of doing things.
  ~ Neil Lewis

Contributors to free and open source software projects may have a day job and they may be able to work on their projects only during weekends. Their job may require them to be online during weekdays, but that does not necessarily mean they are available for a discussion. Depending on the nature of work, they may or may not be able to answer your queries during weekdays. It is thus very important for you to keep a journal of your activities. You can create and update your journal as and when you complete your tasks. Even if you are stuck with a problem, you can write about it in the various communication channels and people might give you solutions. Mentors who are busy during weekdays can see your blog post when they have time and know about your progress. If there aren't any frequent updates, then it is a sign that there is a problem. Also, the blog acts as a tool to showcase your work. You will need to have accomplished some task before you can write something. Search and archives of the posts serve as documentation for you and others. An update must be provided at least once every week.

4.7 Never make your own decisions

We promise according to our hopes and perform according to our fears.
  ~ François de la Rochefoucauld

When you are young and energetic, you have a lot of enthusiasm and interest. But, you have to be cautious about being over-confident. People with experience have immense knowledge that they can guide you well. It is very important to see different points of view before making a decision. Never commit to something without thoroughly analysing the scope and impact of your changes. Always try to seek a second or third opinion. If you have made a decision, you must be 100% sure that you can defend yourself no matter what questions are asked. Research well and do your homework. Some projects have maintainers for specific modules and they are responsible for it. You will need to get their approval before the project can accept your changes. It is thus very important to have a good rapport with your team members. The more you deviate from the goals of the project and make your own decisions, the more you will feel left out. Always consult others when you are new to a project. It takes years of experience to become a master and commander of a project.

4.8 Forget to CC members

Everybody knows everybody, and there is a very high degree of transparency.
     ~ Yossi Vardi

Free and open source software development is a double-edged sword. The openness in the communication tools provides transparency for any dispute that may arise. It is thus very important to have all the project discussions in the respective project mailing lists. You can use private discussions only if you wish to discuss personal matters. If a project team is small and they prefer to use e-mails for communication, it is important to CC every one in the discussion. Forgetting to include members in the discussions will cause confusion among the team members. It is very important for everyone to be on the same page. If your development module affects other projects or consumers of your software, it is important to inform them about any upcoming changes. Always keep everyone informed!

4.9 Repeat same mistakes

```
Go ahead and do what you think is right. If you
make a mistake, you will learn from it. Just
don't make the same mistake twice.
     ~ Akio Morita
```

Working with free and open source software does require you to be a self-starter. The methodology of work is not suitable for everyone. Some people like to be given tasks to work on, and they will follow that strictly. There is nothing wrong with that. But, you should know what your strengths and weaknesses are. Only by accepting your mistakes can you start to think of a solution for the same. You can write about them in your journal or blog so you remember not to repeat them in future. If you do keep committing the same mistakes repeatedly, then the task may not be suitable for your style of work. It is perfectly fine to move on to other tasks or even a different project after informing the respective project team members. It is very normal for people to change projects and domains if they feel there is a need to do so. Repeating the same mistakes is a concern for you and the project.

4.10 Can friends also join the project?

```
"Me and my friend studied in the same school. We
went to the same tuition centre. We joined the
same college and department. Can we work on the
same project?"
```

The friends circle vary in numbers in an institution. It is very common for a group of friends in a class to decide to work together on a project. They usually decide among themselves as to who will work on which part of the project. It might also be the case where only one person actually does the work, and the other team members just support the cause. The transparency in free and open source software projects doesn't encourage the above behaviour. Every project team member's contributions are visible. Each individual has his own clone of the project repository in a decentralized version control system. The individual commits made by them can be observed. The pull requests will let us know whose changes were absorbed, if the work is a contribution to a larger project. While it is fine with friends to work together on a project, it is important to learn to work with people outside your comfort zone. The free and open source software projects enable you to network and work with people from different backgrounds and countries. You need to make the best use of this opportunity. This experience will teach you how to build relationships with newer people in a project. It is acceptable for a group of friends to work together, but, make sure that everybody learns and contributes to the project.

4.11 Commit early, commit often

```
"Code, code, code your way,
 Gently down the screen,
 Commit early, commit often,
 And life is but a dream."
```

One of the main principles of working in free and open source software development is to commit early and commit often. It is easier to correct mistakes at an early stage rather than having to complete the project and present it to users, only to realize that it is not what they had asked for. Project team members who are voluntarily contributing to the project will be able to take time to review smaller changes. If a project has test suites, then the small changes can trigger invocation of test runs and you can detect any failures immediately. When you return from vacation, it takes time for you to recollect what you have been working on the project. If you made commits often, then it will be easy for you to review the changes. If there are dependency modules in a project, then committing often and checking the test runs early can help detect any issues. The concerned users of the project will be able to review the changes and provide any feedback.

This also helps avoid doing any last minute work. Being able to detect problems at an early stage also gives you an opportunity to rectify them, and helps you plan your time and project deliverables.

4.12 Never make assumptions

Question your own assumptions and the assumptions of others.
    ~ Alan Kelly

It is very important to do your homework and provide justification wherever necessary. You should be able to give sufficient arguments in case of a dispute. When building a solution, you must review the steps to ensure that you have all the corner cases addressed. It is also important to be honest, and say "no" if you are not sure. If you decide to work on a new feature request, first attempt a proof of concept (PoC) implementation. Research on the available approaches and do a feasibility study. Learning from others' experience on something which does not work can save you time and effort. In free and open source software development, you are encouraged to use open standards since the specifications are freely available. What works in one proprietary system, may or may not work in other systems. It is thus very important to run tests before you provide a solution. Proofs are not the same as tests though. Review your work to make sure you haven't made any assumptions. If you have, note them down as constraints for the specific implementation.

4.13 Never hesitate to ask questions

The scientist is not a person who gives the right answers, he's one who asks the right questions.
    ~ Claude Lévi-Strauss

There is no question as a stupid question. The more questions you ask yourself, the more you will learn. But, free and open source software project team members may be working voluntarily in a project. It will be wise to do your homework before you ask questions. You can mention the various sources and links that you had referred to, and what you didn't understand in them. It gives an indication that you are serious about solving the problem and are eager to seek answers. You should avoid making direct requests in a mailing list asking for an immediate answer. The list members have no obligation to answer them. They may refer you to an appropriate source of information, or provide you useful links. It is also good to think in terms of the Five Ws and one H (Who, What, When, Where, Why, and How) when researching on a given problem. Always reason, and never hesitate to ask questions.

4.14 Priorities

The most important and basic thing is to learn and understand the needs of a customer.
~ Vinod Gupta

Developers working on free and open source software projects work with a lot of passion and interest. They are more concerned about doing things right even if it takes time. A project may have release schedules where users may expect certain features. In such scenarios, it is necessary to note the priorities of the tasks. Measuring complexity is indeed very hard. Every individual will have a different opinion on the time it will take to complete a task. But, if it is a customer-facing project, understanding the priorities helps in planning your work. You can also assign priorities for sub-tasks that you work on, on a daily or weekly basis. Understanding the users, project requirements, and their importance can help set your priorities right.

4.15 GTD

A bitzui'ist is someone who just gets things done.
~ Dan Senor and Saul Singer

It is very important to do what it takes to get the work done. You should have, of course, done your research and home work before starting on your work. Planning and time management are crucial to keep track of your project work. Doing things in the last minute will reflect poorly. A well thought and planned work can be showcased to others as an example. The following are good books that I recommend on managing your time and work:

- Stephen R. Covey. "The 7 Habits of Highly Effective People." [1]
- Fergus O'Connell. "How to Get More Done: Seven Days to Achieving More." [2]
- Chad Fowler. "The Passionate Programmer." [3]
- Andrew Hunt, and David Thomas. "The Pragmatic Programmer: From Journeyman to Master." [4]
- Kevlin Henney. "97 Things Every Programmer Should Know." [5]

As much as you can do advocacy for a project, you should equally work on the project tasks and get things done.

4.16 References

1. Covey, Stephen R. 2000. *The 7 Habits of Highly Effective People*. Simon & Schuster.

2. O'Connel, Fergus. December 2007. *How to Get More Done: Seven Days to Achieving More*. Prentice Hall.

3. Fowler, Chad. 2009. *The Passionate Programmer*. Pragmatic Bookshelf.

4. Hunt, Andrew, and Thomas, David. 1999. *The Pragmatic Programmer: From Journeyman to Master*. Addison Wesley.

5. Henney, Kevlin. 2010. *97 Things Every Programmer Should Know: Collective Wisdom from the Experts*. O'Reilly Media.

5 Development Guidelines

I do not know of any other technology than programming that is invited to cover a grain ratio of $10^{\char`\~}10$ or more.
    ~ Edsger W. Dijkstra

5.1 Can I do a Java project?

It is not the language that makes programs appear simple. It is the programmer that make the language appear simple!
    ~ Robert C. Martin

A common question among students is about their final year project - "Can I do a Java or Android project?" Students ask such language-specific or technology-related project questions because they feel they will get a job in the same language or technology. If the only programming language you know ceases to exist, does that mean you will lose your job? You need to learn to think in terms of problems and domain knowledge where you wish to solve problems, and not programming languages. Your attitude and problem-solving skills should help you work in any programming language in any domain.

5.2 Math and Engineering

Engineering isn't about perfect solutions, it's about doing the best you can with limited resources.
    ~ Randy Pausch

Given a problem, students tend to proceed directly to the computer, open their favourite text editor, and start coding. There are two sides to a coin - math and engineering. It is important to understand the problem, the logic for the solution, and prove it is correct before proceeding for an implementation. The math remains the same, while the engineering implementation can differ among people and programming environments. If there are any logical errors in the program, the math will help you analyse the same.

5.3 Programming Paradigms

There are different programming paradigms that exist today - procedural, object-oriented, functional and logic. Most students have read and programmed in either one or two of them. It is good to learn to think and program in the different paradigms. Even if you don't use all of them, learn how they approach problems and tackle them in distinct ways. It will open up your mind to solving problems differently.

```
No programming paradigm works equally well along the
axes of performance, domain complexity and scale.
     ~ Larry O'Brien
```

5.4 The Big main() function

```
Divide and conquer.
```

I have often observed students solving a problem inside a single main() function, whether C, C++, or Java. It is one big main() function that runs into hundreds of lines of code. The following is a sample C program written by a student for matrix addition:

```c
#include <stdio.h>

int main(int argc, char **argv)
{
int a[3][3], b[3][3], c[3][3], i, j;

for (i=0; i<3; i++)
{
for (j=0; j<3; j++)
{
a[i][j] = 0;
}
}

for (i=0; i<3; i++)
{
```

```
for (j=0; j<3; j++)
{
b[i][j] = 0;
}
}

printf ("3x3 Matrix addition\n");

printf ("Enter the first matrix:\n");

for (i=0; i<3; i++)
{
for (j=0; j<3; j++)
{
scanf("%d", &a[i][j]);
}
}

printf ("Enter the second matrix:\n");

for (i=0; i<3; i++)
{
for (j=0; j<3; j++)
{
scanf("%d", &b[i][j]);
}
}

for (i=0; i<3; i++)
{
for (j=0; j<3; j++)
{
c[i][j] = a[i][j] + b[i][j];
}
}

printf ("Sum of matrices:\n");

for (i=0; i<3; i++)
{
for (j=0; j<3; j++)
```

```
{
printf("%d ", c[i][j]);
if (j == 2)
  printf ("\n");
}
}

return 0;
}
```

If the code is not indented, it then becomes difficult to read. The application of logic, and the use of functions and classes in practical code must come from the thought process. Since the entire code doesn't fit in a screen, it also becomes difficult to test or debug the same. You must learn to divide the problem into sub-problems, and write individual functions for each. The above code could have been written as follows:

```
#include <stdio.h>

#define DIMENSION 3

void
matrix_init (int x[][DIMENSION])
{
  int i, j;

  for (i=0; i<DIMENSION; i++)
    {
      for (j=0; j<DIMENSION; j++)
        {
          x[i][j] = 0;
        }
    }
}

void
matrix_read (int x[][DIMENSION])
{
  int i, j;
```

```
    for (i=0; i<DIMENSION; i++)
      {
        for (j=0; j<DIMENSION; j++)
          {
            scanf("%d", &x[i][j]);
          }
      }
}

void
matrix_add (int x[][DIMENSION], int y[][DIMENSION],
       int z[][DIMENSION])
{
  int i, j;

  for (i=0; i<DIMENSION; i++)
    {
      for (j=0; j<DIMENSION; j++)
        {
          z[i][j] = x[i][j] + y[i][j];
        }
    }
}

void
matrix_print (int x[][DIMENSION])
{
  int i, j;

  for (i=0; i<DIMENSION; i++)
    {
      for (j=0; j<DIMENSION; j++)
        {
          printf("%d ", x[i][j]);

          if (j == DIMENSION - 1)
            printf ("\n");
        }
    }
}
```

```
int
main (int argc, char **argv)
{
   int matrix_one     [DIMENSION][DIMENSION];
   int matrix_two     [DIMENSION][DIMENSION];
   int matrix_result  [DIMENSION][DIMENSION];

   matrix_init( matrix_one    );
   matrix_init( matrix_two    );
   matrix_init( matrix_result );

   printf ("3x3 Matrix addition\n");

   printf ("Enter the first matrix:\n");
   matrix_read( matrix_one );

   printf ("\nEnter the second matrix:\n");
   matrix_read( matrix_two );

   matrix_add( matrix_one, matrix_two, matrix_result );

   printf ("\nSum of matrices:\n");
   matrix_print( matrix_result );

   return 0;
}
```

The compilation and sample execution of the above program with the GNU C Compiler is given below:

```
$ gcc matrix.c -o matrix

$ ./matrix

3x3 Matrix addition
Enter the first matrix:
1 1 1
1 1 1
1 1 1
```

```
Enter the second matrix:
2 2 2
2 2 2
2 2 2

Sum of matrices:
3 3 3
3 3 3
3 3 3
```

5.5 Copyright header, license

Free Software projects use the GNU General Public License where the copyright notice and license information need to be included in the sources. A GPLv3 header in a source code is shown below:

```
This program is free software: you can redistribute
it and/or modify it under the terms of the GNU
General Public License as published by the Free
Software Foundation, either version 3 of the
License, or (at your option) any later version.

This program is distributed in the hope that it
will be useful, but WITHOUT ANY WARRANTY; without
even the implied warranty of MERCHANTABILITY or
FITNESS FOR A PARTICULAR PURPOSE. See the GNU
General Public License for more details.

You should have received a copy of the GNU General
Public License along with this program.  If not,
see <http://www.gnu.org/licenses/>.
```

Refer the GPL HOWTO guide [2] for more details on how to use it in your programs. It is essential to decide the license you wish to use for your project and mention it in your sources. If you use multiple software components released under different free and open source software licenses, you will need to check for license inter-operability. If you decide to use any third-party software, you will need to request permission for use and abide by their terms and conditions.

5.6 Validate user input

When you read input from a user or from an external device or from some third-party source, it is required to validate the same. A programming problem or assignment may not state it explicitly, but, it is expected of you to ensure that it is safe to use the data. Any corrupt data can cause devastating effects during program execution.

Suppose you wish to use a 6-digit postal code in your application in the form "411013". The following regular expression in the Ruby programming language can be used to validate the same:

```
^\d{6}$
```

The input can be given in various forms - "411 013", "four one one zero one three", or "411-013". A successful match for the regular expression returns the position of the match, while, a nil is returned for no match. A simple iteration in the Interactive Ruby Shell (irb) to test the regular expression with examples is shown here:

```
$ irb

irb(main):001:0> "411 013" =~ /^\d{6}$/
=> nil

irb(main):002:0> "411-013" =~ /^\d{6}$/
=> nil

irb(main):003:0> "four one one zero one three" =~ \
irb(main):004.0*      /^\d{6}$/
=> nil

irb(main):005:0> "411013" =~ /^\d{6}$/
=> 0
```

5.7 Exception handling

Any logic that you implement must handle corner cases that may arise during program execution. If you decide to abort in the middle of a function, you must make sure to clean up anything that has already been set up. When dealing with input from a network or any I/O device, exception handling must be used.

If you wish to operate on a file, you need to check if the file exists, and it is indeed a file and not a directory. If you also want to read from it, you need to check if you have the necessary access permissions. The following example in Ruby displays the contents of a file if it exists and is also readable:

```ruby
#!/usr/bin/env ruby

def file_contents(file)
  if File.exists?(file)
    if File.file?(file)
      if File.readable?(file)
        puts File.read(file)
      else
        puts "#{file} is not readable!"
      end
    else
      puts "#{file} is not a file!"
    end
  else
    puts "#{file} does not exist!"
  end
end

file_contents('/home/guest/.bashrc')
```

5.8 Test cases

The use of small functions allows one to write unit tests, and also test them with examples. By running the tests you get the confidence that your code actually works. It also helps in debugging code by isolating the function that causes any problem. Some free and open source software projects also emphasize the need for functional and integration tests. Different programming languages have test libraries and frameworks that you can use to test your code. Learn to use them well. The following even.py Python code has a simple function to check if a given number is even or not:

```python
#!/usr/bin/python

def is_even(n):
    """
    Returns true if number 'n' is even
    """
    return n % 2 == 0
```

The Python test.py file to test even.py is given below:

```python
#!/usr/bin/python

import unittest
import even as e

class IsEvenTests(unittest.TestCase):

    def test_false(self):
        self.assertFalse( e.is_even(1) )

    def test_true(self):
        self.assertTrue( e.is_even(2) )

def main():
    unittest.main()

if __name__ == '__main__':
    main()
```

The execution of the tests is shown here:

```
$ python test.py
..
-----------------------------------------------------
```

```
Ran 2 tests in 0.000s

OK
```

```
Write programs that do one thing and do it well.
    ~ Douglas McIlroy
```

5.9 Build tools

```
The build should compile and perform its unit tests
within about ten minutes.
    ~ James Shore and Shane Warden
```

The compilation, build, test, packaging steps for a project need to be automated as much as possible. The Autotools [3] GNU build system assists in making software projects portable across platforms. GNU Make [4] and CMake [5] are tools that use Makefiles to automate tasks. These help to avoid any typing mistakes when you do manual compilation. Continuous integration tools like Jenkins [6] and Travis CI [7] can run project tests and create nightly builds on different platforms. These can also be used for document generation. Computer science is all about automation, and learning to use these tools as part of your project is essential. The more you automate, the easier it is to run your test suites. If you are having a deployment production instance, having a development and stage instance can come in handy during testing and migration.

5.10 Learn about your editor

```
The tools of the mind become burdens when the
environment which made them necessary no
longer exists.
    ~ Henri Bergson
```

There have been numerous debates and discussions, online and offline, on the most popular text editor. There is no one single editor of choice. People have their own favourite ice-creams, and none is better than the other. What is important is for you to learn everything that the editor provides you with. Command-line editors are quite powerful too, and it is good to learn at least one. User-friendliness does not mean fancy Graphical User Interfaces (GUI). It means whether the editor can actually be helpful to do what the user needs. Spending considerable time learning to use an editor will help you use it effectively in the long run. There is no silver bullet. You need to try different editors, and choose the one you like - just like ice-cream!

5.11 Touch Typing

In most of my workshops, the lab exercises never get completed. Most students whom I have observed don't know how to touch type. They see the keyboard and type. They then look at the screen to verify what they had actually typed. If they have to type by looking at a book or a sheet of paper, their speed is painstakingly slow. Very few students know how to type in their native language. The speed of typing does not determine the quality of work. But, the faster you type, the faster you can get data into the system.

```
The arrangement (QWERTY) of the letters on a
typewriter is an example of the success of the least
deserving method.
    ~ Nassim Nicholas Taleb
```

The continuous use of the QWERTY keyboard caused a lot of pain, and I was forced to rest my fingers. While it is good to take a break, it shouldn't be done for the wrong reason. Dr. August Dvorak and Dr. William Dealey completed the Dvorak simplified keyboard layout in 1932. I have now switched to using it. If you are not familiar with touch typing, you can begin to learn and use the Dvorak keyboard layout. There exists free and open source software like Klavaro [10] to practice typing. Prepare a schedule for the different levels in the touch typing exercises, allot time every day, and practice regularly until you are able to touch type effectively.

With early typewriters the mechanical arms would
jam if two letters were hit in too rapid a
sequence. So the classic QWERTY keyboard was
designed to 'slow down' typing.
     ~ Edward de Bono

5.12 Triaging

If any bug or problem is reported, the first step is to
reproduce the problem. This is called "triaging", and it is a
very important step. The bug reporter needs to provide as
much information as possible to reproduce the error. The
following is an incomplete bug report:

The program is compiling properly forming a proper
GUI but its not finding the word in an editor and
not running properly.

Learning to write a complete bug report is an art. There
are many useful HOWTOs and documentation available
online [11]. Setting up the environment is the first step to
isolate the conditions that may have caused the problem.

5.13 Documentation

A man who has the knowledge but lacks the power to
express it is no better off than if he never had any
ideas at all.
     ~ Thucydides

Whether you face a problem, or you are nearing completion
for a task or sub-task, it is important to document it
immediately. In future, if you encounter the same error, your
notes will tell you how you had solved the problem. Your
documentation can be your personal diary, a blog, or part of
a project wiki. You can also mention any troubleshooting
steps that you took, or any bug that you encountered, or a
forum post for reference. The more detailed and precise the

information, the better it is for yourself and others on why and how you made decisions or solved issues. By posting it to the project mailing list, you might also get help from others on how you can solve it better. Avoid any last minute documentation as far as possible.

5.14 Experience is the best teacher

Figure: Illustrative proof of $(a+b)^2 = a^2 + 2ab + b^2$

Knowledge gained through rote learning does not last long. I have asked the expansion and proof of $(a+b)^2$ during my workshops, and many students were not able to provide a proof for the same. This is just an example. A simple proof will be to take a line, divide it into two segments - 'a' and 'b', make a square, and compute the areas. The area of the square is $(a+b)^2$, which is the same as the sum of the areas comprising the square, which is, $a^2+ab+ab+b^2 = a^2+2ab+b^2$.

Once you have understood the proof, you will not need to 'mug up' anything, and you will never forget it.

Always reason, and question everything.

```
People don't learn by understanding; they learn by
some other way, by rote or something. Their
knowledge is so fragile.
```

~ Richard Feynman

5.15 References

1. Pausch, Randy. 2008. *The Last Lecture.* Hyperion.
2. GNU General Public License HOWTO. `http://www.gnu.org/licenses/gpl-howto.html`.
3. Autotools - A Practitioner's Guide to Autoconf, Automake and Libtool. `http://fsmsh.com/2753`.
4. GNU Make. `http://www.gnu.org/software/make`.
5. CMake. `http://www.cmake.org`.
6. Jenkins. `http://jenkins-ci.org`.
7. Travis CI. `https://travis-ci.org`.
8. Taleb, Nassim Nicholas. 2005. *Fooled by Randomness: The Hidden Role of Chance in Life and in the Markets.* Random House.
9. Bono, Edward De. 1993. *Serious Creativity: Using the Power of Lateral Thinking to Create New Ideas.* Harperbusiness.
10. Klavaro. `http://klavaro.sourceforge.net/en`.
11. Tatham, Simon. How to Report Bugs Effectively. `http://www.chiark.greenend.org.uk/~sgtatham/bugs.html`.
12. Feynman, Richard. 1989. *"Surely You're Joking, Mr. Feynman!": Adventures of a Curious Character.* W. W. Norton.

6 Methodology of Work

This could be a lesson for some of our software development methodologists: Study software, not software methods.

~ Richard Gabriel

6.1 The initial steps

```
Start young - you will get more time to make
mistakes and rectify them.
        ~ Sunil Gaitonde
```

There are few basics that you must know before you get started with free and open source software projects. There is no silver bullet, but you can follow a systematic approach in your work. The preliminary steps are described below:

6.1.1 Newborn

The newborn stage involves learning to use a GNU/Linux system. Before you start contributing to free and open source software, you need to know how to install and use it. You should also set up your Internet connection, and if there are any network problems, you will need to troubleshoot the same and get them fixed. Configuring and using system and network services are also important. You should also learn to use Internet Relay Chat (IRC). Register your nickname on IRC before using it. You must also create a blog where you can provide regular updates of your work.

6.1.2 Infant

The infant stage is when you learn about the various projects, communication guidelines, and best practices in free and open source software development. History is important and you need to know why the software came into existence. You must read the content on "Free as in Freedom" [1], "How to become a hacker" [2], and "Linux and the Unix philosophy" [3]. You can also browse online for other reading material on the subject. There are a couple of excellent documentary movies that you can watch - "Revolution OS" [4] and "The Code Linux" [5].

6.1.3 Toddler

In the toddler stage, you need to learn to use the command line interface. You need to spend time learning the shell commands and the shell environment. The "UNIX Concepts and Applications" book by Sumitabha Das [6] is highly recommended. You will also find plenty of tutorials online that you can refer to. You need to be able to navigate the file system, and execute basic shell commands. With practice and experience, you will be able to write useful shell scripts. The use of connectors such as pipes illustrate the *nix philosophy of doing one thing, and doing it well. Bash is available on most GNU/Linux distributions, but you can explore other shells like zsh [7], ksh [8] and csh [9]. You may not always have a fancy Graphical User Interface (GUI) to work with, and hence learning to use the command line interface can come in handy. It is also useful when you have to work remotely, and when you don't have the required network bandwidth for viewing GUIs. The power of the shell is truly unimaginable.

6.1.4 Kid

The next phase is the kid stage where you select a project of your choice and start work on it. You will need to learn the programming language, revision control software, project workflow, documentation and other tools used in the project. As you gain experience, you will become an expert. You should continue to seek advice from the project team members and community as you work on your tasks. Adhere to the project guidelines to ensure that the best practices are followed.

6.2 Bug fix example

Solving bugs is a good way to get started in a project. You will focus only on one small component of the project, but, it will help you learn the tools and workflow used in the project. Consider the bug "661714 - typo in answer to 'What are file contexts?' question" [10]. The bug has been reported for the selinux-faq documentation, where there is a duplicate entry in the SELinux_FAQ.xml file:

```
<option>relabel</option>, <option>relabel</option>
```

You first need to locate the selinux-faq documentation sources. After searching online, you will find the following relevant links at:

```
http://fedoraproject.org/wiki/SELinux_FAQ
```

```
http://docs.fedoraproject.org/en-US/Fedora/13/
html/SELinux_FAQ/
```

The code is available at:

```
https://fedorahosted.org/web/
```

The relevant file that has the duplication is present in:

```
http://svn.fedorahosted.org/svn/selinux-faq/
community/trunk/en-US/SELinux_FAQ.xml
```

The project uses Subversion for managing the code repositories. Assuming that you are new to the project and the tools, you first need to learn how to use Subversion (svn). There are two types of documentation - HOWTOs and reference manuals. You need to know when to use which type of documentation. Assuming that you are new to Subversion, you can start with a tutorial or user guide. Before you can make any changes to the documentation you need a copy of the project. After reading and understanding about Subversion, you will come to know that the 'checkout' option allows you to get a copy of the project. If you don't have the tool available in your GNU/Linux distribution, you will need to install it first. On Fedora, for example, you can install using:

```
$ sudo yum install subversion
```

If the user does not have sudo access, check with your distribution documentation on how to provide the user with the security privileges. To checkout the sources, use:

```
$ svn checkout \
    http://svn.fedorahosted.org/svn/selinux-faq/
```

Publican is used for documentation, and so you proceed to read on using it. Install the software on your GNU/Linux distribution. On Fedora, you can use:

```
$ sudo yum install publican
```

In order to generate the HTML pages, the following command needs to be invoked from the trunk/ directory:

```
$ publican build --formats=html --langs=en-US
```

In the tmp/en-US/html/index.html page, you will notice the observed bug. Since you don't have access to the actual web server that hosts the web pages, you will need to submit a patch with the appropriate fix. You can treat this checkout as a working copy. Open trunk/en-US/SELinux_FAQ.xml using your favourite text editor, and replace one of the 'relabel' text with 'restore' and save it. You can then produce the diff output and re-direct it to a patch as shown below:

```
$ svn diff
Index: SELinux_FAQ.xml
===================================================
--- SELinux_FAQ.xml (revision 47)
+++ SELinux_FAQ.xml (working copy)
@@ -298,7 +298,7 @@
 <para>
   Fedora ships with the <command>fixfiles</command>
   script, which supports four options: <option>
   check</option>,
-  <option>relabel</option>, <option>relabel
-  </option> and
+  <option>restore</option>, <option>relabel
+  </option> and
   <option>verify</option>. This script allows users
   to relabel the file system without having the
   <filename>selinux-policy-targeted-sources
   </filename>package installed. The command line
   usage is more friendly
```

```
$ svn diff > bug-661714-use-restore.patch
```

The bug-661714-use-restore.patch file can then be submitted for bug 661714 as an attachment in Bugzilla for review. Do not hesitate to check the manual page or documentation for a software or tool for help.

6.3 Packaging example

CBMC [11] is a static analysis bounded model checker for ANSI-C and C++ programs. The current build process downloads the minisat2 [12] module from the Internet, and is required for compilation. As a package maintainer, it is required to use the libraries and tools provided by the distribution. Hence, the build process needs to be modified.

You first need to download the CBMC sources from their website. They use Subversion for managing the code releases, and you need to have it installed first before you can checkout the sources. On Fedora, you can do:

```
$ sudo yum install subversion
$ svn checkout \
    http://www.cprover.org/svn/cbmc/releases/cbmc-4.6
```

Read the COMPILING file in the sources to see how to compile the package. The following dependencies are required for compilation. On Fedora, you can use the following:

```
$ sudo yum install gcc gcc-c++ flex bison \
    make zlib-devel
```

Download the SAT solver as mentioned in the COMPILING file in the sources:

```
$ cd src
$ make minisat2-download

Downloading Minisat 2.2.0
Saving to 'minisat-2.2.0.tar.gz'...
```

```
42.9 KB received in 1 seconds (42.9 KB/sec)
```

Compile the source:

```
$ make
```

If you have all the dependencies available in your distribution, the CBMC source will compile. In order to remove the dependency on downloading minisat2, and to use the Fedora shipped minisat package, you will need to read about Makefiles. Learning about autotools will also be helpful. You can use the book on "Autoconf, Automake and Libtool" [13] to get started. Install the required dependencies if not available:

```
$ sudo yum install minisat2-devel
```

After understanding about Make, Fedora packaging, you will do the following changes in a copy of the source directory to use the system installed minisat2 libraries.

```
Index: src/cbmc/Makefile
=====================================================
--- src/cbmc/Makefile    (revision 3284)
+++ src/cbmc/Makefile    (working copy)
@@ -22,7 +22,7 @@

 INCLUDES= -I ..

-LIBS =
+LIBS = -lminisat

 include ../config.inc
 include ../common
Index: src/common
=====================================================
--- src/common   (revision 3284)
+++ src/common   (working copy)
@@ -23,8 +23,8 @@
 else
```

```
   EXEEXT =
 endif
-  CFLAGS ?= -Wall -O2
-  CXXFLAGS ?= -Wall -O2
+  CFLAGS = ${RPM_OPT_FLAGS}
+  CXXFLAGS = ${RPM_OPT_FLAGS}
   CP_CFLAGS = -MMD -MP
   CP_CXXFLAGS = -MMD -MP -DSTL_HASH_TR1
   #LINKFLAGS = -static
Index: src/config.inc
=====================================================
--- src/config.inc    (revision 3284)
+++ src/config.inc    (working copy)
@@ -11,7 +11,7 @@
 #CHAFF = ../../zChaff
 #BOOLEFORCE = ../../booleforce-0.4
 #MINISAT = ../../MiniSat-p_v1.14
-MINISAT2 = ../../minisat-2.2.0
+MINISAT2 = /usr/include/minisat
 #GLUCOSE = ../../glucose2.2
 #SMVSAT =

Index: src/goto-instrument/Makefile
=====================================================
--- src/goto-instrument/Makefile    (revision 3284)
+++ src/goto-instrument/Makefile    (working copy)
@@ -28,7 +28,7 @@

 INCLUDES= -I ..

-LIBS =
+LIBS = -lminisat

 CLEANFILES = goto-instrument$(EXEEXT)

Index: src/solvers/Makefile
=====================================================
--- src/solvers/Makefile    (revision 3284)
+++ src/solvers/Makefile    (working copy)
@@ -17,7 +17,7 @@
 ifneq ($(MINISAT2),)
```

```
  MINISAT2_SRC=sat/satcheck_minisat2.cpp
  MINISAT2_INCLUDE=-I $(MINISAT2)
- MINISAT2_LIB=$(MINISAT2)/simp/SimpSolver$(OBJEXT) \
+# MINISAT2_LIB=$(MINISAT2)/simp/SimpSolver$(OBJEXT) \
  $(MINISAT2)/core/Solver$(OBJEXT)
  CP_CXXFLAGS += -DHAVE_MINISAT2 \
  -D__STDC_FORMAT_MACROS -D__STDC_LIMIT_MACROS
  override CXXFLAGS := \
       $(filter-out -pedantic, $(CXXFLAGS))
endif
```

Test the same using:

```
$ cd src
$ make
```

If you want to be a packager, you need to go through the Fedora packaging guidelines [14] and workflow involved.

6.4 Software development

Retask [15] is a distributed task management Python module. You can obtain the sources from https://github.com/kushaldas/retask. If you don't have git installed on your system, install it. On Fedora, for example, you can do:

```
$ sudo yum install git
$ git clone git://github.com/kushaldas/retask.git
```

The SHA1 version returned from the checkout is f4d823827bed0545818eca39f0ab1238ea0aa95b. Redis [16] is required to use retask, and you can install it on Fedora using the following command:

```
$ sudo yum install redis
```

You can start an instance of the Redis server by opening another terminal and running:

```
$ redis-server
```

You first need to install the dependencies for Retask, and check if you can run the tests. If you do not have Python installed in your system, install it. On Fedora, you can do:

```
$ sudo yum install python
```

Enter into the sources directory for Retask, and run the tests as shown below:

```
$ cd retask
$ python tests.py

Traceback (most recent call last):
  File "tests.py", line 3, in <module>
    from mock import patch
ImportError: No module named mock
```

An error occurs, and you should not panic. So, the mock package is not installed on the system. Searching for mock using your distribution package manager yields python-mock. Install it and try again:

```
$ sudo yum install python-mock
$ python tests.py
....
--------------------------------------------------
Ran 4 tests in 0.006s

OK
```

One of the TODO tasks is to list all the queue names. They begin with the prefix "retaskqueue-". You can now make a copy of the sources for your development, or create a git branch to implement this feature. You can first add your code and experiment with the Python interpreter to make sure your code works. If you are new to Python, go through some online reading material to learn the language. The following code is added in retask/queue.py:

```
def names(self):
    data = ""
    if not self.connected:
        raise ConnectionError('Queue not connected')

    try:
        data = self.rdb.keys("retaskqueue-*")
    except redis.exceptions.ConnectionError as err:
        raise ConnectionError(str(err))

    return data
```

You can now proceed to test the code directly with the Python interpreter:

```
retask $ python -m retask.queue
retask $ python
Python 2.7.3 (default, Aug  9 2012, 17:23:57)
[GCC 4.7.1 20120720 (Red Hat 4.7.1-5)] on linux2
Type "help", "copyright", "credits" or "license"
for more information.
>>> from retask import Queue
>>> from retask import Task
>>> q = Queue('foo')
>>> q.connect()
True
>>> entry = {'user':'shakthimaan',
>>> ... 'url':'http://www.shakthimaan.com'}
>>> task = Task(entry)
>>> q.enqueue(task)
<retask.queue.Job object at 0x7fb824e891d0>
>>> q.names()
['retaskqueue-foo']
```

You can also add a unit test function to tests.py.

```
class GetQueueNamesTest(unittest.TestCase):
    """

    Gets a task in the Queue
```

```
    """
    def setUp(self):
        queue = Queue('lambda')
        queue.connect()
        t = Task({'name':'kushal'})
        queue.enqueue(t)

    def runTest(self):
        queue = Queue('lambda')
        queue.connect()
        results = queue.names()
        self.assertEqual(results[0],
                              'retaskqueue-lambda')

    def tearDown(self):
        rdb = redis.Redis()
        rdb.delete('retaskqueue-lambda')
```

Executing the tests gives:

```
retask $ (master) python tests.py
.....
----------------------------------------------------
Ran 5 tests in 0.007s

OK
```

The complete patch with the necessary changes can be submitted upstream for review:

```
---
 retask/queue.py | 12 ++++++++++++
 tests.py        | 20 ++++++++++++++++++++
 2 files changed, 32 insertions(+)

diff --git a/retask/queue.py b/retask/queue.py
index c292e43..7e28d4b 100644
--- a/retask/queue.py
+++ b/retask/queue.py
@@ -58,6 +58,18 @@ class Queue(object):
```

```
          self.rdb = None
          self.connected = False

+   def names(self):
+       data = ""
+       if not self.connected:
+           raise ConnectionError('Queue not connected')
+
+       try:
+           data = self.rdb.keys("retaskqueue-*")
+       except redis.exceptions.ConnectionError as err:
+           raise ConnectionError(str(err))
+
+       return data
+

      @property
      def length(self):
          """
diff --git a/tests.py b/tests.py
index 07316c4..268f3b9 100644
--- a/tests.py
+++ b/tests.py
@@ -64,6 +64,26 @@ class GetTest(unittest.TestCase):
          i = task.data
          self.assertEqual(task.data['name'], 'kushal')

+class GetQueueNamesTest(unittest.TestCase):
+     """
+     Gets a task in the Queue
+
+     """
+     def setUp(self):
+         queue = Queue('lambda')
+         queue.connect()
+         t = Task({'name':'kushal'})
+         queue.enqueue(t)
+
+     def runTest(self):
+         queue = Queue('lambda')
+         queue.connect()
+         results = queue.names()
```

```
+          self.assertEqual(results[0],
+                          'retaskqueue-lambda')
+
+    def tearDown(self):
+        rdb = redis.Redis()
+        rdb.delete('retaskqueue-lambda')

 if __name__ == '__main__':
     unittest.main()
--
```

1.8.1.4

6.5 References

1. Williams, Sam. March 2002. *Free as in Freedom: Richard Stallman's Crusade for Free Software*. O'Reilly Media. http://oreilly.com/openbook/freedom.

2. Raymond, Eric Steven. 2001. *How to become a hacker*. http://www.catb.org/esr/faqs/hacker-howto.html.

3. Gancarz, Mike. 2003. *Linux and the Unix Philosophy*. Digital Press. http://www.amazon.com/Linux-Unix-Philosophy-Mike-Gancarz/dp/1555582737.

4. Revolution OS. http://www.revolution-os.com.

5. The Code Linux. http://www.code.linux.fi.

6. Das, Sumitabha. 2006. *UNIX Concepts and Applications*. Mcgraw-Hill Education. http://www.amazon.in/UNIX-CONCEPTS-AND-APPLICATIONS-Sumitabha/dp/0070635463?tag=googinhydr15928-21.

7. zsh. http://www.zsh.org.

8. ksh. http://www.kornshell.com.

9. csh. http://en.wikipedia.org/wiki/C_shell.

10. *Bug 661714 - typo in answer to 'What are file contexts?' question*. https://bugzilla.redhat.com/show_bug.cgi?id=661714.

11. CBMC. http://www.cprover.org/cbmc/.

12. minisat2. http://minisat.se/MiniSat.html.

13. Autotools - A Practitioner's Guide to Autoconf, Automake and Libtool. `http://fsmsh.com/2753`.

14. Fedora packaging. `https://fedoraproject.org/wiki/Packaging:Guidelines`.

15. Retask. `https://github.com/kushaldas/retask`.

16. Redis. `http://redis.io/`.

7 Tools

The whole is equal to the sum of its parts.
  ~ *Euclid*

7.1 History

```
Anyone who closes his eyes to the past is blind to
the present.
    ~ Richard von Weizsäcker
```

The tools used in free and open source software development exist for a reason. They are there to help get work done. It is very important for you to understand the history behind a tool's existence, and why it is used in a project. You may have used other tools in your previous projects, but working with free and open source software is a different experience and you need to learn to use the tools effectively. As much as it is important to use the right programming language to solve a kind of problem, it is important to use the right communication tool for the right job, with the right people at the right time. Students often tend to choose a programming language of their choice, and then decide to do a project using it. Choose the tool that best helps solve a problem. Understanding the need for a particular tool can help you better to grasp its use in a project.

7.2 Blog

```
It is not good to be a scientist unless you think
that it is of the highest value to share
your knowledge.
    ~ Robert Oppenheimer
```

A blog is a journal of posts that can be useful for documentation and reference. It is very important to blog regularly, at least once every week. Status updates and announcements can be made on your blog. When working on a project, it is good to do a weekly blog report to your

mentor. It ensures that you do some work to be able to write
an update, and it also helps you to improve your writing
skills. RSS (Rich Site Summary) feed for your blog can be
easily passed around, and your viewers can easily subscribe
to it. They primarily use pull technology, and a number of
blog readers exist that can help you subscribe to feeds. A
collection of blogs can be aggregated. Planet [1] software
allows you to collect and display feeds from various websites.
Fedora Planet [2] in an example.

7.3 E-mail

```
A sentence should contain no unnecessary words for
the same reason that a drawing should have no
unnecessary lines.
    ~ E B White
```

E-mails are a common form of communication, and can be
a distraction at work. It is important to check them only
periodically, otherwise, you can easily get carried away with
them. The context switch from checking e-mails to getting
back to what you were doing earlier is at least 10 minutes.
It is also important to not get entangled with flame wars
in mailing lists, as they tend to drain your energy and
time. If you feel that the discussion is veering away from
the actual topic, try not to add fuel to the fire. Always try
to adhere to the topic of discussion, and avoid making any
personal comments. E-mail clients can be used from the
browser, command line, or a standalone application such
as Thunderbird [3]. You can also choose to synchronize
e-mails from multiple servers and read them offline using
OfflineIMAP [4].

7.4 Forums/Mailing lists

Forums and mailing lists are two different ways of having
interactions on a project. Some projects have separate
mailing lists for user and developer discussions. For
example, fedora-list is for users, while, fedora-devel is
developer-centric. Some projects have separate mailing
lists for announcements too. It is important to join all the

mailing lists for a project that interests you. People who use command-line e-mail clients, generally prefer using mailing lists. Forums are more web intuitive and are common among end users. Even if you don't actively participate in the mailing lists and forums, reading the discussions can help you learn from them.

```
Every difference of opinion is not a difference
of principle.
    ~ Thomas Jefferson
```

7.5 Internet Relay Chat

```
It ain't just what you say [content], it's the way
that you say it [form].
    ~ Gordon Rugg and Marian Petre
```

Discussions also occur through Internet Relay Chat (IRC). Each project has an IRC channel where conversations happen. It can be considered as a form of online technical support where you can ask questions. Both technical and non-technical discussions crop up in these channels. If people are online, they might answer your queries, or they may be away from the keyboard (AFK). Being patient is important. You can also write to the mailing list of a project if you don't get a reply in the channel. You should create a unique IRC nickname, and register with the IRC server, so that others know that it was you who had logged in every time in the channel. There are a number of IRC clients available that you can use to connect to the servers. XChat [5] is an example.

7.6 Messenger Chat

```
One sometimes finds what one is not looking for.
    ~ Alexander Fleming
```

Messenger chats are text-based, instant messaging software that are suitable for one-on-one conversations. These require you to add your friends to your contacts before you can start a conversation. These too can be a distraction at work. Some of them have support for using webcams, sharing files between two parties, and sending offline messages. They may also provide native language support. The messenger clients can connect to multiple chat networks that use different communication protocols. Pidgin [6] is an example. Use instant messaging sparingly.

7.7 Voice chat

```
The simple act of speaking is a known elixir for
treating an unclear mind.
   ~ Chad Fowler
```

Ekiga [7] is a free and open source video conferencing software for voice chats. If a project team requires to have an online video conference then this tool can be used. Different users might have different Internet connectivity bandwidth, and this might affect the quality of the video. You need to make sure that the relevant firewall ports are not blocked to allow video transmission. Voice chat does require the full user's attention during the meeting. Try to keep this usage to a minimum, or use it only when the project team needs to resolve major issues.

7.8 Wiki

Project documentation can be written using Wikis. This allows different project members to share their documentation. These can be reference manuals or tutorials. It is important to write documentation for future reference not just for yourself but for others as well. A project documentation may include notes on installation, usage, testing, feature requests, developer HOWTO, troubleshooting, FAQs etc. It is important to go through the documentation of a project before you start work on it. MediaWiki [8] is a popular example of a Wiki. You can also set up a Wiki instance on your local machine for your documentation needs. Since the software is available, you can do customization as per your needs.

Knowledge is of two kinds. We know a subject
ourselves, or we know where we can find information
upon it.
   ˜ Samuel Johnson

7.9 Pastebin

We only think when we are confronted with a problem.
   ˜ John Dewey

Pastebin web services are useful to share code snippets,
errors and log output. When you submit your text to the
web service, it will return a URL that you can pass to IRC
channels for people to have a look at. Paste URLs have a
time period for which they are valid, and they can vary from
an hour, to a day, or even a month. Example of such services
include fpaste [9], and GitHub gist [10]. Some of them have
syntax highlighting support to neatly format the output for
a specific programming language. Learn to use them when
you have problems in your work, and when you want to
share the relevant code or text to others for troubleshooting.

7.10 Ticketing/Bugs

If you can do something about a particular issue,
do it.
   ˜ Fergus O'Connell

A project needs to keep track of the work and bugs filed
for different versions of the software. Free and open source
software ticketing systems such as Bugzilla [11], Trac [12], and
Mantis [13] exist. These require you to create an account for
authentication before starting to use their service. It will be
good to learn to use these tools effectively. These can also
be a starting point for selecting newbie tasks to begin with.
The user interfaces may vary among the tools, but, spend
some time to understand the workflow used by the project
team. If some bugs have deadlines and are assigned to you,

you need to complete them on time. A release might have a set of features and a deadline, and you need to give them the highest priority. Do ensure to have notifications in place to send you updates on new bugs, or you must review the list of bugs periodically.

7.11 Editors

To write is human, to edit is divine.
    ~ Stephen King

The editor is a very important tool that is part of your work. It could be a command line editor, or an Integrated Development Environment (IDE), or it could be the browser. Whichever user interface you use, make sure you learn as much of the capabilities provided by the tool. It is something that you are going to be spending a lot of time on, to get your work done, and mastering it is very essential. Command line editors are powerful too, and it is good to know at least one. You can create a quick reference card to refer any shortcuts that you use. Editors also allow you to tailor their settings. Make sure to have a backup of your customizations online, or carry them on a USB thumb drive so that you can use them on other computers as well.

7.12 Version Control Systems

Those who cannot remember the past are condemned to repeat it.
    ~ George Santayana

The use of version control systems is very important and should be part of your everyday work. Whether it is code or documentation, you should be able to review your work periodically, and also be able to undo and redo them easily. Hence, learning to use a version control system is essential. Today, decentralized version control tools like Git [14] and Mercurial [15] help you to keep copies of your work on multiple systems. While these tools don't force you to follow a specific workflow, it is essential for you to know the basics.

You can read on how others are using the tool, and create your own custom workflow. Keeping copies of your project work on remote servers and backing them up can come in handy. If there are newcomers to a project, the revisioning and smaller commits made can help them learn about the development and progress made in the project. Spend quality time learning to use these tools, and use them every day in your work.

7.13 Build tools

A project may use many programming languages, frameworks, libraries, and software suites. The entire process of translating source into machine code or to make it ready for production deployment may involve several build steps. It is important for you to learn the build tools that are associated with a project. Makefiles [16] are common and are written to build software. There are a number of other build tools like SCons [17], Maven [18], and CMake [19]. There can also be project specific frameworks with customized tools to build artefacts for users. It is thus important for you to learn these tools, workflows and the processes used in the project.

```
Make it run, then make it right, then make it fast.
   ~ Kent Beck
```

7.14 Publishing tools

```
A picture is worth a thousand words.
```

When you use images in your project, you may want to resize, modify or transform them and you will need to learn to use image manipulation tools like GIMP [20]. If you are designing badges, posters, or need vector graphics images, learning to use Inkscape [21] is essential. If you are in the publishing industry, you will need to master Scribus [22]. These tools can come in handy not just for documentation purpose, but, for any presentations that you want to make. Spend quality time going through their tutorials and manuals, and learn to use them well.

7.15 Others

You won't improve without change; you won't undergo
change without pain.
       ~ Gordon Rugg and Marian Petre

While it is important to learn to use the various tools used in a project, it is also essential to be open to exploring new tools. You should have the knack to pick up new tools if they are introduced in a project for various reasons. People do try to look for free and open source software equivalents for proprietary software. There are no equivalents because the freedom given to you with source code is priceless, and there is no room for comparison. The development cycle may be fast, and you must be quick to adapt to any changing environment and tools. Learning is a never-ending and continuous process.

7.16 References

1. Planet. http://www.planetplanet.org.
2. Fedora Planet. http://planet.fedoraproject.org.
3. Thunderbird.   http://www.mozilla.org/en-US/thunderbird.
4. Offlineimap. http://offlineimap.org.
5. XChat. http://xchat.org.
6. Pidgin. http://pidgin.im.
7. Ekiga. http://ekiga.org.
8. MediaWiki.   http://www.mediawiki.org/wiki/MediaWiki.
9. fpaste. http://fpaste.org.
10. GitHub Gist. https://gist.github.com.
11. Bugzilla. http://www.bugzilla.org.
12. Trac. http://trac.edgewall.org.
13. Mantis. http://www.mantisbt.org.
14. Git. http://git-scm.com.

15. Mercurial. `http://mercurial.selenic.com`.

16. Makefiles. `http://www.gnu.org/software/make/manual/html_node/Makefiles.html`.

17. SCons. `http://www.scons.org`.

18. Maven. `http://maven.apache.org`.

19. CMake. `http://www.cmake.org`.

20. GIMP. `http://www.gimp.org`.

21. Inkscape. `http://inkscape.org/en`.

22. Scribus. `http://www.scribus.net/canvas/Scribus`.

8 Reading and Writing

If you want to be a writer, you must do two things above all others: read a lot and write a lot.
   ~ Stephen King

8.1 Terminology

```
This business of journalism is about pure
entertainment, not a search for truth.
   ~ Nassim Nicholas Taleb
```

When you belong to a group, it is important to understand and learn the values of the group and what they believe in. It will help you become associated with the group. The meaning of the word "hacking" is to engage in activities to improve on what already exists. The hack will reflect your caliber and excellence to fellow people. Hackers are people who want to push technology to the forefront, and are eager to solve challenging problems [1].

```
What they had in common was mainly love of
excellence and programming. They wanted to make
their programs that they used be as good as they
could. They also wanted to make them do neat things.
They wanted to be able to do something in a more
exciting way than anyone believed possible and show
"Look how wonderful this is. I bet you didn't
believe this could be done."
   ~ Richard Stallman
```

The term "hacker" has been misinterpreted in many circles. People who break into systems and bring down networks are called "crackers". It is thus important to know and use the correct terminology when you belong to these circles. It is also important to make people aware of the history of such terminology when it is being misused. In engineering circles, hacking is still considered development work. Also, the free software movement is different from the open source software movement. Some are only free software contributors, while others are part of the open source software movement. There are people who participate in both the movements. It is thus important to understand the ideals of a group to be a part of it.

8.2 Types of documentation

Documentation can be of different types and can come from different sources. In the free and open source software world, you will find two major types of documentation - reference manuals and HOWTOs. A chapter or a section in a reference manual can be read directly without having to read the previous chapters. You do not have to read it like a book, from start to finish. A manual for a software can differ depending on the version of the software. A HOWTO document starts from point A and ends in point B. You will need to go through it from the beginning till the end. The objective will not be met if you skip some steps in between or start from somewhere in the middle of the document. You should know when to use which type of documentation, and also be open to refer various documentation sources for information. If you do not understand the content by an author, try to read the same subject written by other authors. You will see how they have expressed the same subject in a different manner. You will be able to get a wholistic picture and a better insight when you read from multiple sources.

```
If ... a sentence still reads awkwardly, then what
you have there is an awkward sentence. Demolish it
and start again.
     ~ Keith Waterhouse
```

8.3 Online search

It is important to spend time reading online. If you wish to learn on a topic, you can use a search engine for the same. You can also collate the information and keep the links for reference, or, write a document or blog post about it for future reference. This approach requires you to be a self-starter and it is important when working in free and open source software communities. You can also search and read forums and mailing lists. You can also subscribe to online blog posts and Planet [2] feeds for information. What is important is that you do your homework, and read documentation before trying them out. Knowledge does not come to you, but you will need to seek it.

```
It's the method that's important, never mind if you
don't get the right answer.
    ~ Tom Lehrer
```

8.4 Illegal downloads

Students prefer to download e-books from the Internet that explicitly specify that the book is protected by copyright, and that it should not be shared freely. Students need to be made aware of copyright, patents and trademark. As a result, this behaviour is also prevalent in their computer lab work, where they have a tendency to copy programs and submit them without following any license. Some universities do use plagiarism software to check for content duplication. Students also have a tendency to copy verbatim from Wikipedia without citing references. I believe that when you invest in buying a book, you will at least read it once for the money that you have spent on it. Making people aware of piracy and encouraging the use of free and open source software and standards is an important approach to break this behaviour.

```
In the process of gaining our rightful place we must
not be guilty of wrongful deeds.
    ~ Martin Luther King Jr
```

8.5 Newspaper

I ask students in my workshops if they have the habit of reading newspapers, and few of them raise their hands. I then ask how many of them read only the first and last pages of a newspaper, and most of their hands are still raised. The typical answer is that they don't have time to read an entire newspaper. It is important to keep yourself up-to-date with what is happening around you. It does not matter whether you read the news online or offline, but, it is important to read. It is common for free and open source software enthusiasts to travel to different countries, and learn about different cultures. General knowledge is as important as technical know-how. While news can be biased or used for propaganda, it is important to distinguish between them and draw a line as to how much time you intend to spend. But, do inculcate the habit of reading the news!

```
Personally I am always ready to learn, although I do
not always like being taught.
   ~ Sir Winston Churchill
```

8.6 Reference books

```
I'll tell you right now that every aspiring writer
should read The Elements of Style.
   ~ Stephen King
```

You should keep a good collection of reference books. Whether you use an e-book reader or you buy a printed version, these reference books will always come in handy. Whether it is your workplace or your home, keeping a collection is important. There are also pocket reference guides available that you can carry with you when you are travelling. They provide a concise summary of tools, languages, content and usage and are ideal for quick reference. A hard cover bound book will last you for many years when compared to a paperback. The quality of paper used in a book also matters. It is good to keep a personal copy of reference books, so that you can refer them whenever you want to.

8.7 Library membership

It is good to be a member of a library where you can get a wide collection of books. It can either be offline or online. It can cater to a large audience, or it can be used for technical reference. But, you must seek out for information and thus becoming a member in at least one library is important. Libraries also organize occasional events and activities where you will meet people from different backgrounds, and you can make friends who have common interests in reading books, or are interested in your area of work. Online library access for books may require you to have an Internet connection. Some do offer reference books for reading for a stipulated period of time. Learn the different services offered in your library membership, and use it effectively.

```
Science is more than a body of knowledge; it is
a way of thinking.
   ~ Carl Sagan
```

8.8 Motivational reading

```
I have nothing to offer but blood, toil, tears
and sweat.
   ~ Sir Winston Churchill
```

There are times when you may feel let down in life. Reading non-fiction and motivational books will help you boost your self-confidence. The book by Dale Carnegie on "How to stop worrying and start living" [3] can be read many times and can teach you many important lessons in life. It is also good for you to read biographies and auto-biographies of people to see how hard they have worked to come up in life, and how they have tackled hardships. I highly recommend the following books:

- Ioan James. "Driven to Innovate." [4]
- Alan Axelrod. "Winston Churchill CEO: 25 Lessons for Bold Business Leaders." [5]
- Atul Gawande. "Better." [6]
- Akio Morita. "Made in Japan - Akio Morita and Sony." [7]
- Srijan Pal Singh, A. P. J. Abdul Kalam. "Target 3 Billion." [8]

- Dan Senor, Saul Singer. "Startup - Nation." [9]
- David A. Vise and Mark Malseed. "The Google Story." [10]
- Randy Pausch. "The Last Lecture." [11]
- Joel N. Shurkin. "Broken Genius: The Rise and Fall of William Shockley." [12]
- Dale Carnegie. "How to Win Friends and Influence People." [13]
- Andrew Stellman, Jennifer Greene. "Beautiful Teams." [14]

8.9 Writing

```
The ratio of time spent reading vs. writing is well
over 10:1.
   ~ Robert C. Martin
```

Sharing knowledge is a very important aspect in the free and open source software community. The written form of communication is widely used to share content. You must actively contribute to this medium for others to review your work and give you a feedback. Participating in mailing lists and forums can also help you gain knowledge. You should have a blog where you can write about your work. You can also write for magazines, and some of them pay you a honorarium. You can create an outline for a topic, and list down the various sections you want to write on, and use a pad, paper and pen or pencil. After entering the content on to a computer, you can review the draft and make a final version. If you are interested in writing a book, there are publishers who can offer you assistance, or you can decide to self-publish. The joy of sharing is part of the free and open source software community, and writing regularly and consistently is very important.

8.10 Notes taking

A lecture or workshop may provide you with handouts that you can refer to later. Some points discussed during a talk may not be available in the notes, and you may want to scribble them down. It is important to write legibly, so that you may understand your own handwriting. You may also forget what the speaker is saying when you are taking down notes. It is thus important to write whatever you want, and you must do so quickly. The same is applicable for classroom lectures. You can take a picture of your written document for future reference, or, you may wish to type them fully. Using a freehand may be helpful, especially, when you want to quickly draw diagrams. Taking down notes needs a lot of experience and practice. When you are reading books online, the text copy feature may be disabled, and hence you will not be able to copy the relevant text. You can decide to note them down for future reference.

In our schools, reading, writing, and arithmetic are practiced as skills that detach the child from sensory experience.
    ˜ Rudolf Arnheim

8.11 Writing technique

Writing is an act of faith, not a trick of grammar.
    ˜ E B White

Your handwriting is very important. Otherwise, you yourself will not be able to understand what you have written. This is important if you are taking notes in a classroom or in a lecture. Stephen King recommends in his book "On Writing" [15] that your first draft must be written with the doors closed. You can review the text with the doors open. It is important to review your writing at least three times, or until you are satisfied. Do not hesitate to re-write if you feel like. You can look at your draft after giving yourself a break, and with a fresh mindset. You should also review your writing when in a different mood. This will bring out a different perspective in the way you have written. Do use a revision control tool to keep copies of your earlier drafts. You should not throw away any written content, as they may be required in the future.

8.12 Books on improving writing

After I had read poetry for a year or so, my
technical and scientific writing got much better.
~ Richard Gabriel

A number of books can help you improve your writing.
The book on "Good English: How to Write It" [16] by
G. H. Vallins is a good one to start with. If you want
an overall idea about the art of writing, Stephen King's
book on "On Writing" [15] is excellent. It does address
writing for fiction as well. You will also need to keep
books on grammar for reference. The "High School English
Grammar & Composition" [17] book by Wren and Martin
is recommended if you wish to review your grammar and
usage. The other must-have books in your collection are
the Skunk's "The Elements of Style" [18] and "English
Composition and Grammar" [19] by John E. Warriner. You
can also provide your writing work to your close friends and
associates and ask them for their opinions. You can also
use professional editorial services to give you an assessment,
provided they don't disclose the contents to others without
your consent.

8.13 Dictionary and thesaurus

All the words I use ... can be found in a
dictionary - it's just a matter of arranging them
in the right order.
~ Somerset Maugham

A sound vocabulary will help you in your writing and
communication. You must make every effort to improve
your vocabulary. A strong command of the language can
help in your conversation with other people. If you do not
understand the meaning of a word, check with a dictionary.
It is good to keep a hard copy for quick reference, or, if you
are connected to the Internet, you can check the meaning
online. You should also check the usage of the word, and
the various forms that it can be used in. You should also

invest in a thesaurus, especially if you spend time writing, as this will be useful for you to look at alternative words and their usage. Before you publish any document, you must run a spell-checker tool for the entire document. A good dictionary can come in handy if you need to check the correct spelling and meaning of words.

8.14 Time allotment

```
If you don't have time to read, you don't have the
time (or the tools) to write. Simple as that.
    ~ Stephen King
```

You need to allocate time for reading and writing. The more you read, the better your knowledge. But, you should not spend all your time just reading. You will need to produce work, and writing is one means to prove yourself. The quality of contents read will also reflect on the quality of work produced. Plan in advance on how much time you will spend for both reading and writing. Measure the time using any time-tracking tool and see how you perform. Stephen King suggests in his book "On Writing" [15] that you need to learn to read in sips. You may not be able to finish an entire chapter at once, but, learning to read whenever you have time will help you complete it.

```
Reading is the creative center of a writer's life.
The trick is to teach yourself to read in small sips
as well as in long swallows.
    ~ Stephen King
```

8.15 References

1. Hackers: Wizards of the Electronic Age. http://www.handtap.com/hackers.

2. Planet. http://www.planetplanet.org/.

3. Carnegie, Dale. 1990. *How to Stop Worrying and Start Living*. Pocket Books.

4. James, Ioan. 2009. *Driven to Innovate*. Peter Lang Ltd.

5. Axelrod, Alan. 2009. *Winston Churchill, CEO: 25 Lessons for Bold Business Leaders.* Sterling Pub Co Inc.

6. Gawande, Atul. 2008. *Better.* Picador.

7. Morita, Akio. 1998. *Made in Japan - Akio Morita and Sony.* Signet.

8. Pal Singh, Srijan, and Kalam, A. P. J. Abdul. 2011. *Target 3 Billion.* Penguin India.

9. Senor, Dan, and Singer, Saul. 2011. *Startup - Nation.* Twelve.

10. Vise, David A. and Malseed, Mark. 2005. *The Google Story.* Delacorte Press.

11. Pausch, Randy. 2008. *The Last Lecture.* Hyperion.

12. Shurkin, Joel N. 2008. *Broken Genius: The Rise and Fall of William Shockley.* Palgrave Macmillan.

13. Carnegie, Dale. 1998. *How to Win Friends and Influence People.* Pocket Books.

14. Stellman, Andrew and Greene, Jennifer. 2009. *Beautiful Teams.* O'Reilly Media.

15. King, Stephen. 2010. *On Writing: A Memoir of the Craft.* Scribner. http: / / www . stephenking . com / library/nonfiction/on_writing:_a_memoir_of_the_craft. html.

16. Vallins, G. H.. 1952. *Good English: How to Write It.* PAN.

17. Wren, P.C, and Martin, H.. 1995. *High School English Grammar and Composition.* S. Chand Publishing.

18. Strunk Jr., William and White, E. B. 1999. *The Elements of Style.* Longman.

19. Warriner, John E. 1988. *English Composition and Grammar.* Harcourt Brace Jovanovich.

9 Art of Making Presentations

The human brain starts working the moment you are born and never stops until you stand up to speak in public.
  ~ *Sir George Jessel*

9.1 Stage

```
Only those who will risk going too far can possibly
find out how far one can go.
    ~ T. S. Elliot
```

Some students do have a stage fright and are shy to make a presentation even to their classmates. Some of them have a language and communication problem that creates a fear in them that their friends might ridicule them. Faculty do allow two or three students to work together on a project, but, only one gets chosen to present the project work to the class. It is good to have regular talks in the classroom, and students must take turns for the same. Only with experience will they gain the confidence to speak to an audience. You can also record your session and then play it back to see how you could have presented it better. You can start with lightning talks that last a few minutes before you can give regular talks for a longer duration.

9.2 Microphone

```
Awareness is closely related to cognition; action is
closely related to behaviour.
    ~ John Mason and Kaye Stacey
```

An audience in a small hall will be able to hear you without a microphone if your voice is loud enough. If your sessions last for long hours or a day at least, your throat may become sore the following day. As far as possible, try to use a microphone to speak to your audience. This also gives the facility to record the sessions for future playbacks. It is very important to hold the microphone at the right distance from your mouth so that your voice is not too loud. Learn to speak softly. Listen to your voice from the speaker output, and control the pitch and scale of your voice. Before you start using the microphone, every time, check with the audience whether you are audible enough, even at the last row in the hall. Also, before you answer a question, you should repeat the question for the benefit of all.

9.3 Visual Equipment

He who controls the present controls the past, and he who controls the past controls the future.
    ~ George Orwell

A video projector may be required for your presentation. It is important for you to go early to the venue to test your laptop with the projector. Sometimes, the cable may be at fault and a particular colour may not show up. Other times, the required screen resolution may not appear. You will need to request the organizers to keep a standby projector in case you are not able to use your system with the allotted one. You should also request them for a computer or laptop with the required GNU/Linux distribution installed that has been tested with their projector. You must also have a copy of your slides in a USB thumb drive, so that you can use the standby computer if your system is not compatible with the projector. You should be prepared to deliver your presentation even without a projector. For example, the blackboard and chalk, or whiteboard and markers can be used for explanation while the slides can be shared via USB or through the network to the participants. It is of utmost importance that you should also test the Internet connectivity at the venue before you begin your session. You can also save the required web pages and show them offline.

9.4 Dress Code

In free and open source software community, quality of work is given more importance than your appearance, but, it is good to be presentable when you are addressing an audience. Even though there is no formal dress code, some conferences may expect you to have a formal attire, and it is good to dress appropriately, respecting the values of the occasion. Your objective should be to deliver the content and reach out to the audience, and they shouldn't be distracted by your dress. Some do choose to maintain an uncommon dressing style as their trademark so that they can easily be identified in a larger crowd, or if they belong to a particular clan or group. It is also good to carry an extra set of dress if you are travelling. If you are attending workshops in cold countries, or travelling abroad, do check the weather conditions prevailing there and take the appropriate clothing to protect yourself.

```
Judge a man by his questions rather than by
his answers.
    ~ Voltaire
```

9.5 Audience

```
Build yourself into a brand, an identity that marks
you as both unique and valuable.
    ~ Alan Axelrod
```

It is important for you to look into the eyes of your audience and speak to them. It may not be possible in a large auditorium, especially if lights are on you, but, you must regularly observe how attentive your audience is. Do try to give your audience a break, at least once every hour. If you are able to move away from the stage and mingle with the audience, doing so will have a personal touch and will also make them comfortable. You can also ask them a few questions and make the session interactive, depending on the nature of the topic and the objective of your session. If you find them restless, seek their attention immediately. Before you start preparing for a talk, identify the target audience to whom you will be addressing, and what their expectations might be. When on stage, if you realize that the audience needs are different, ask them for their expectations, and scale your talk accordingly. There must be a message that your audience should take home at the end of your session.

9.6 Tone

```
I have never heard the equal of Hardy for clarity,
for interest, or for intellectual power.
   ~ Norbert Wiener
```

Speakers who are inexperienced have a habit of reading the text from the slides. They might also read them in a monotonous way. You need to listen to the tone of your voice when you speak to your audience. You can also record the audio, play it back to see how you can improve it. You can prepare a set of points and the order in which you wish to present them. You can then expand them, and write a transcript that you can revise and use. You may also practice by presenting the same in front of a mirror. If you are too shy to present the talk at a conference, you can first attempt to present the same to your friends, or classmates, or in your local GNU/Linux user group meetings. Based on the feedback, you can then improve upon your presentation skills, and this will also help boost your self-confidence. This approach can greatly help people who stammer a lot and who have stage fright.

9.7 Data and Presentation

```
Text is more efficient at dealing with large amounts
of content because of data abstraction.
   ~ Mike Gancarz
```

Data and presentation should be kept separate. Tools like Pandoc [1] allow you to represent text in markup, and they can be exported to different formats like HTML, PDF, and EPUB [2]. This also ensures extensibility, as supporting a new output format will only require writing a plugin for the same. You can revision control your text and build configuration settings. Depending on the content and how long you intend to maintain the sources, you can also decide to use WYSIWYG tools for your presentations. Visual designers who like to use the mouse prefer this approach.

But, separating data from presentation for large volumes of text will scale well, and can be easily maintained.

9.8 Formats

Somehow, as an industry, we fool ourselves thinking market leader is the same thing as standard.
    ~ Chad Fowler

One of the principles behind using free and open source software is the encouragement and use of free and open standards. It is good to practice what you preach. Try to use open standard formats and tools for your presentations. This will ensure that your content will stand the test of time as long as the standards exist. If you use proprietary tools, you are then dependent on the vendor, and if they don't provide backward compatibility, you will end up spending a lot of time re-working your presentations, or even having to maintain multiple versions of the document for different versions of the software. Use free and open source software documentation tools like LibreOffice [3], LaTeX [4], Texinfo [5], Asciidoc [6], Pandoc [1], or Publican [7] for your documentation work.

9.9 Content

You must look at facts because they look at you.
    ~ Sir Winston Churchill

Do your homework on a subject before you decide to make a presentation. See what content is already available on the topic. Get to know about the target audience to whom you are going to present the topic. Write an objective for the presentation and what you wish to achieve from it. An abridged version of a presentation can also be helpful for you and others to improve it later. You can decide to split a topic into multiple presentations and vary the depth of the content for different durations. You can also make detailed presentations for a topic depending on the type of the audience and its interests. If a particular content becomes outdated, make sure to update the slides and release a new, revised version. You can also provide a Rich Site Summary (RSS) [8] feed for your presentations if you decide to make frequent releases.

9.10 Meta content

```
Always include your data source in your graphics.
It not only provides credibility but also context.
     ~ Nathan Yau
```

You can start your presentation with an eye-catching statement or an illustration. But it is important to provide necessary references for your content. If you decide to use an image from another web page or source, make sure that it can be re-used, or you will need to request permission from the author. Try to provide as many links to Uniform Resource Locators (URLs) [9] in your content so that interested readers can check them for more information. You will need to mention the license under which your presentation will be released. You should also provide your name and contact e-mail address in the presentation. It will be good to include a version number in your presentation, to identify newer versions from earlier releases. If you have uploaded your presentation online and circulated the URL in various mailing lists, it is good to review any feedback provided on the same for improvement.

9.11 Slides

```
I want to know God's thoughts, the rest are details.
     ~ Albert Einstein
```

The number of slides in a presentation can vary depending on the time you intend to spend on each slide. Avoid too much of text in your slides. You might reduce the font size to fit all the text in a slide, but, when projected on a screen, the audience seated in the last row may not be able to read it. Try to use as many illustrations as possible. Do not leave a lot of white space as it might get unnecessary attention of the viewer. Some templates may include the author name and presentation title in every slide. You can periodically show the outline of your slides to indicate where you are in the presentation. Always provide a reference section at the end of the presentation with links. If you have taken a picture or excerpt from the web, mention the source at the bottom of the slide. Rehearse your transcript with the slides and time your sessions so that you can manage your presentation on the day of your talk.

9.12 Workshops

```
Getting involved means activity: heads down,
hands dirty.
     ˜ John Mason, Leone Burton, and Kaye Stacey
```

The hands-on sessions can be a different experience as compared to delivering a lecture. While a talk can have an element of suspense or surprise, it will be helpful to send a list of sessions to be worked upon in a lab. If there is any software or system setup that is required, the steps need to be sent to the participants prior to the workshop. This will also help them focus on the actual workshop content and not waste time trying to set up their systems. If the participants need to use the Internet, the connectivity must also be checked before the sessions begin. If slides or data need to be used during the workshop, a network file sharing setup needs to be done. It will be a strain to use the computer continuously for long hours, and hence it is recommended to take regular breaks. Depending on the typing speed and capability of the individuals, the workshop tasks may or may not get completed. It is essential for you to keep a track of the time and decide to move the sessions forward. The participants can take notes and follow-up with the tasks after the end of the session or do it as homework.

9.13 Question & Answer

The presentation that you make may be interactive or you may choose to have the question and answer (Q&A) session at the end of your talk. Some people may want to get their doubts clarified before you proceed to the next slide, and may decide to ask you a question. Using your discretion and depending on what background information you need to provide, you may decide to answer the question then and there itself. If you feel that it will be relevant to answer the question after addressing few forthcoming topics, you can answer the question at a later stage. If you feel that the question is beyond the scope of your current session, you can decide not to answer it or take it offline. If you are not sure, you can choose to refer different sources and come back with answers after the workshop. An interactive session will be lively for the audience, but, you must keep an eye on the time to ensure that you cover all the points that you intended to cover in your sessions.

```
Questioning everything means you are no longer
taking the status quo as truth.
   ~ Robin Sharma
```

9.14 Failover

```
Success is the ability to go from one failure to
another with no loss of enthusiasm.
   ~ Sir Winston Churchill
```

You should request the audience to put their mobile phones in silent mode so that it doesn't distract you and others during the presentation. It isn't uncommon for things to go wrong during a presentation. A power failure may deprive you from using the projector. You should immediately shift to the whiteboard or blackboard and use markers or chalk to present your talk. You can also use this time to explain theory and concepts. If you are presenting at a conference, and if the audience has a different set of expectations, some may decide to leave the hall. You should not get distracted by movement of people. Whatever happens, you must make every effort to get your message to the audience. Due to commuting problems, if you arrive late at the venue, try to re-schedule your sessions according to the importance and expectations of the audience. At any given time, if you face hindrances, you should be able to step up to the task and deliver your presentation. With experience, you will be able to master the art of making and delivering excellent presentations.

9.15 References

1. Pandoc. `http://johnmacfarlane.net/pandoc`.

2. EPUB. `http://idpf.org/epub`.

3. LibreOffice. `http://www.libreoffice.org`.

4. LaTeX. `http://www.latex-project.org`.

5. Texinfo. `http://www.gnu.org/software/texinfo`.

6. Asciidoc. `http://www.methods.co.nz/asciidoc`.

7. Publican. `https://fedorahosted.org/publican`.

8. Rich Site Summary (RSS). `http://www.rssboard.org`.

9. Uniform Resource Locator. `http://tools.ietf.org/html/rfc3305`.

10 Sustenance

All that is necessary for the triumph of evil is that good men do nothing.

~ *Edmund Burke*

10.1 The three axes

Sustenance is defined in the Oxford dictionary as "the maintaining of someone or something in life or existence". There are three major players in an academic environment - management, faculty and students. They can be represented in a three-dimensional graph where the origin represents an ideal ecosystem where everyone supports free and open source software. I have observed that only one or two of the entities are engaged in promoting the same for a short period of time. Ideally, you should have the backing of all of them. It should not stop you from doing what it takes to learn and improve yourself. The amount of freedom granted in an institute can also greatly affect the survival of free and open source software on campus. Although the software is free ("free as in freedom") [1], proper planning and investment can assist in continuous learning for students, help in their career ambitions and boost the reputation of the institution.

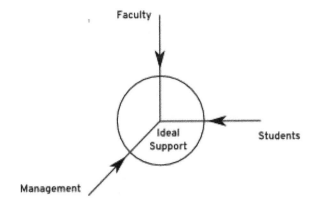

Figure: The three axes

10.2 Infrastructure

Most colleges have high-speed Internet connectivity. They can set up GNU/Linux distribution mirrors to facilitate faster local installations and upgrades. Of course, the lab administrators will need to know how to manage the systems and networks. A faculty with a similar interest can also support and help maintain the free and open source software labs. They can also act as a contact between the management and the lab administrators for resolving any issues. They should be equipped to set up and manage their own services required by the department and the institution. This can vary from setting up a Dynamic Host Configuration Protocol (DHCP) server to managing a Moodle [2] instance for course work. Expensive rack or blade servers are not necessary for the labs. Commodity hardware is sufficient to get started. The use of USB flash drives, CDs and DVDs is usually permitted in the college labs. If students have laptops, they should be allowed to use them in the campus.

```
The Analytical Engine has no pretensions to
originate anything. It can do whatever we know how
to order it to perform.
     ~ Lady Lovelace
```

10.3 The Freedom Lab

```
May we think of freedom, not as the right to do
as we please, but as the opportunity to do what
is right.
     ~ Peter Marshall
```

A college or university must have a lab ("Freedom Lab") where students can do any installation (software/hardware), configuration and testing. This lab need not have expensive machines, but, off-the-shelf hardware can be used. Learning to install hardware, software and troubleshoot problems can help students understand why things fail or succeed. This environment gives them an experimental platform to practice whatever they have read. The ability to restore the system no matter what fails in software, without any liability, gives the students the freedom to learn. Hardware failures need to be fixed. The lab must have access to the Internet and all the network ports must be enabled. This will allow students to play with their own system and network setups.

10.4 Website

Diamonds are not very beautiful in the raw state.
It is the skill of the diamond cutter that reveals
the beauty of the diamond.
    ~ Edward

The first impression is always the best impression. The home page of an institution's website gives a first impression to those who have not visited the campus. The servers hosting the website are usually tightly controlled and secured. Most often they are permitted to use HTML pages only. This is fine, but, with Cascading Style Sheets (CSS), the web sites can be designed well. They don't necessarily have to be dynamic pages. An individual from the college who is a user interface designer or has interest in it can help with the look and feel of the website. An online presence is vital in today's world, and making yourself known to others can help reach out to the outside world. The news and announcement pages must be updated periodically. Departments can have their websites as sub-domains to the top-level college domain. Information on free and open source software projects that students and faculty have worked on can also be provided on the website for others to know more about them. The content in the website should not be articulated for marketing, but, must reflect the contributions made by individuals.

10.5 Tools

There are two parts to learning craftsmanship:
knowledge and work.
    ~ Robert C. Martin

Companies that work in free and open source software are in great need of good engineers. The software projects or components that they use are usually available online in code hosting sites like GitHub [3] or Gitorious [4] or in project specific web sites. In order to showcase your competence, you need to have your contributions in these hosted sites. These add value to the individual and to the institute where they belong. A college or department can also setup its own code repositories using software like Gitorious or Gitolite [5].

Wiki instances for documentation or PlanetPlanet [6] for blogs can be set up in an institute to make their online presence felt in the community. When employers see that you already know how to use the tools of the trade, it is easier for them to make an assessment. When many students contribute to a project, visibility increases considerably with more possibilities of partnerships. Industry-academia collaboration can be a symbiotic relationship. Mailing lists and other software project tools can also be set up for students to interact and learn. These can be made open for outsiders to participate as well. There can exist multiple tools used by a project, but, learning to use them effectively can help prove your talent to the world.

10.6 Conferences

A number of free and open source software conferences are organized every year and it is advisable to attend and learn from those events. The participants are usually from academia, industry, government and the general public. It is a wonderful opportunity to meet the people with whom you have interacted online using the various communication tools. It is also where you match their real names with their Internet Relay Chat (IRC) nicknames. The perspective of a person with whom you have interacted online will be very different when you meet them face-to-face. International speakers will also be present in these conferences and you can get to learn more from their experiences.

The only way to learn is from experience.
    ~ John Mason, Leone Burton, and Kaye Stacey

Networking with people can greatly help in building your contacts. With a lot of experience attending conferences, you must aim to make presentations at these conferences. This will again add value to your profile. With a growing interest

from students and with the support from management and
faculty, it will then be possible for you to start your own
user group in your college and organize monthly meet-ups.
With experience and interest, you could also proceed to host
your own conference. In a given year, if there is a batch of
students who are very enthusiastic about free and open source
software, the next batch of students may not necessarily have
the same interest. Hence, the support of management and
faculty play an important role.

10.7 Budgeting

```
Most local investors believe that without tolerating
large number of failures, it is impossible to
achieve true innovation.
    ~ Dan Senor
```

Budgeting can affect the availability and use of resources.
Embedded hardware, for example, can be expensive. But,
investment must be made periodically on new hardware for
learning. It will be good for every student to have at least
one embedded hardware from which they can experiment,
learn, and take it with them at the end of their study
years. Availability of latest hardware must be guaranteed
by institutions. One must also invest regularly in reading
material for gaining more knowledge. Having a set of
reference books can come in handy. Conferences may have
an entry ticket fee, but, their planning starts early and the
dates are also announced in advance. You can decide on
the conferences you wish to attend in a year and budget
accordingly. Some of them also sponsor the travel and
accommodation for the speakers. If your college is willing to
reimburse your travel expenses, do give them sufficient time
to make a decision. If you are not able to obtain funds from
one source, try contacting the free and open source software
project you are working with for the same. While money is
essential, it must be spent wisely.

10.8 Faculty attrition rate

Many students from engineering colleges graduate every year. While some move to the industry for work, others go for higher studies. When compared with students, faculty and management continue to remain in the institute for longer periods. They need to play an active role in sustaining free and open source software. There are students who don't get an industry job and hence join colleges to teach. After a few years, they try again to get a job in the industry and decide to leave the institute. When this cycle repeats, there is a regular lack of teaching staff in the department. This should not happen. In Finland, for example, only the best are chosen as faculty to ensure that the next generation is taught well [7]. While the faculty attrition rate is a concern for the department, students should not use this as an excuse to not learn by themselves.

```
The number one goal of teachers should be to help
students learn how to learn.
   ~ Randy Pausch
```

10.9 Inter-departmental projects

```
Interdependence is a higher value than independence.
   ~ Stephen R. Covey
```

The scope of a problem may vary depending on the project, and may require people with different areas of specializations to work together. Bioinformatics is an example. Free and open source software projects have no barriers and is an opportunity for you to work on different domains. Students and faculty from different departments can collaborate together to work in such areas. Trying to understand the terminology in a new field, interacting with people from different backgrounds and working to provide innovative solutions in such cross-domain environments can be challenging. The experience gained from such projects will be very valuable though.

10.10 Sources of information

Learning is a continuous and never-ending process. Regular
guest lectures on various subjects of interest can help
shed new light from an outsider's perspective. Attending
workshops and conferences can help you know the current
state of affairs. Multiple sources of reading material, both
online and offline are essential. Periodic review of the
existing collection of books need to be done on a regular
basis. College departments can set up an instance of
Koha [8] to manage their library. Subscription to technical
magazines can give a different viewpoint on a subject. The
important point is that one must not rely on a single source
of information.

```
Knowledge is power.
    ~ Sir Francis Bacon
```

10.11 Certificates

```
It is not your endowment that makes you rich - but
rather hard work.
    ~ Nassim Nicholas Taleb
```

Students always have a keen interest for certification. Inter-
collegiate competitions are held across cities, at the district
level, state level and at the national level. Students see having
certificates as a source of recognition. When working with
free and open source software, there is only one competing
level - international. Your work should be a testament for you
and you shouldn't require any certificate. The work delivered
to the project and your value addition alone should suffice to
the project team and others of your capabilities. Focus on
taking in more work and getting things done. Job, title and
money will come eventually. Learning should be your prime
objective and everything else is just a side effect.

10.12 Hackathons

Hackers are people who push technology to the forefront and are eager to solve challenging problems [9] [10]. Hackathon sessions involve hands-on work with free and open source software projects. These are different from the laboratory sessions that are part of a regular college coursework. Each session can focus on a specific project and they can be scheduled during weekdays or weekends. Depending on the interest, students can form special interest groups for the projects and have regular development sprints. Internet connection and access to Internet Relay Chat (IRC) will be useful. Contributors from existing projects can be invited to guide and oversee the hackathon sessions. Students can also participate in online and offline competitions to gain experience. These are not limited to just programming events, but, can be poster design contests using free and open source software.

```
Learning to write clean code is hard work. It
requires more than just knowledge of principles
and patterns. You must sweat over it.
    ~ Robert C. Martin
```

10.13 Entrepreneur

```
Entrepreneurs' businesses usually grow out of their
passions - and the successful ones nourish them.
    ~ Neil Lewis
```

When your contributions to free and open source software projects grow, you will gain knowledge. As the number of users of the project increases, there may be more feature requests. With generation of new ideas, students can plan to start their own business ventures. Although source code is free, you can offer support, training and customization services. There are different business models that you can adopt. Entrepreneurial workshops can be organized to help students acquire business acumen. The ideas need not necessarily be extraordinary, but, even something small-scale that solves a useful problem is worth an attempt. Networking in conferences can help in obtaining good contacts to improve your business and also improve your technical know-how. Self-sustenance is vital in a society where one needn't always depend on others.

10.14 Sponsored projects

All business, politics, diplomacy is personal, and the most effective leaders are the ones who have always realized this.
~ Alan Axelrod

Companies may develop and release software under a free and open source software license. If they sponsor a project, it is important to clearly distinguish between business and community work. Openness and transparency are very important for the benefit of all. If the ownership of a company sponsoring a project changes hands, the future of that project may be at stake. The parent company may or may not have an interest in that project. Usually, a non-profit organization is constituted with a board of members to govern the project. Some projects require you to transfer copyright ownership to the project. Your contributions will only be accepted after you have transferred ownership. Other projects have a contributor license agreement that you need to accept before you are given access to the project repositories. Read and understand the contract agreements, if any, before deciding to work on a sponsored project.

10.15 Advocacy

The best way to learn is to teach.
~ Robin Sharma

Contributions to a project can be manifold - code, documentation, testing, translation, bug fixing, artwork, troubleshooting users' problems etc. Advocacy is also important. Creating awareness among people on free and open source software can help motivate them to work on it.

You shouldn't force it on them though. Advocacy alone is also not sufficient. One needs to be able to balance time spent on promoting the project with working on project tasks and getting things done. Teaching other people about the project can help you refresh the basics. Answering project related questions can bring a different perspective to the project. Sponsored projects may provide goodies that you can distribute for promotional reasons. While it is good to have them, if available, one must not rely on them entirely. Your focus must always be on the content of the presentation and the quality of the project work.

10.16 Commitment

```
Successful execution of a plan requires absolute
determination and the full vigor of an
unswerving commitment.
    ~ Alan Axelrod
```

A very enthusiastic batch of students will help in organizing meet-ups, inviting guest speakers and attending conferences. Their experience will help them in getting funds or participating in funded projects in the industry like the Google Summer of Code [11]. While participation and completion of a task adds value to the individual, it is important for the individual to continue to work for the project. In low context cultures, people who decide to work in a particular area of interest, work in the field for their entire life. If they decide on a chosen career, they focus their attention on that one profession and work to become an expert in that area.

Unfortunately, in high context cultures, students do get carried away with what is shown in movies, where the 'hero' has to perform many acts - fight, sing, dance, do romance and comedy. In real life, it doesn't work like that though. Being consistent is very hard and to do it for years takes a lot of persistence, determination and hard work. There are students who work in a project, just for the money and stop working once they receive the payment. An employer investing in an individual will like to see long-term commitment from the individual. It takes a lot of resolve to contribute to a project for many years without getting distracted, but, every effort needs to be made to keep the momentum going. As long as there is immense interest and full commitment, sustenance will not be a problem and you will prevail.

10.17 References

1. Stallman, Richard. 2002. *Free as in Freedom: Richard Stallman's Crusade for Free Software. `http://oreilly.com/openbook/freedom/`.

2. Moodle. `https://moodle.org`.

3. GitHub. `https://github.com`.

4. Gitorious. `https://gitorious.org`.

5. Gitolite. `http://gitolite.com/gitolite`.

6. PlanetPlanet. `http://www.planetplanet.org`.

7. LynNell Hancock. 2011. *Why are Finland schools successful?* `http://www.smithsonianmag.com/people-places/Why-Are-Finlands-Schools-Successful.html`.

8. Koha. `http://www.koha.org`.

9. Raymond, Eric Steven. *How To Become A Hacker.* `http://www.catb.org/esr/faqs/hacker-howto.html`.

10. Stallman, Richard. *Hack, Hackers and Hacking.* `http://oreilly.com/openbook/freedom/appb.html`.

11. Google Summer of Code. `https://developers.google.com/open-source/soc`.

www.ingramcontent.com/pod-product-compliance
Lightning Source LLC
LaVergne TN
LVHW092009050326
832904LV00002B/40